There's Nothing Funny about Design

David Barringer

PRINCETON ARCHITECTURAL PRESS

Published by
Princeton Architectural Press
37 East Seventh Street
New York, New York 10003

For a free catalog of books, call 1.800.722.6657.
Visit our website at www.papress.com.

Editor: Linda Lee
Cover design: Felix Sockwell
Book design: David Barringer

Special thanks to: Nettie Aljian, Bree Apperley, Sara Bader,
Nicola Bednarek, Janet Behning, Becca Casbon, Penny (Yuen
Pik) Chu, Russell Fernandez, Pete Fitzpatrick, Wendy Fuller,
Jan Haux, Clare Jacobson, Aileen Kwun, Nancy Eklund Later,
Laurie Manfra, Katharine Myers, John Myers, Lauren Nelson
Packard, Jennifer Thompson, Paul Wagner, Joseph Weston,
and Deb Wood of Princeton Architectural Press
—Kevin C. Lippert, publisher

Library of Congress Cataloging-in-Publication Data
Barringer, David, 1969–
There's nothing funny about design / David Barringer.—1st ed.
   p. cm.
ISBN 978-1-56898-828-3 (pbk. : alk. paper)
1. Graphic arts. I. Title.
NC997.B285 2009
741.6—dc22

                                                   2008040190

LIFE HAS ONLY ONE END—SO DULL.
I WISH YOU MANY BEGINNINGS, LIKE A DREAM.

EYE LIFE: AN INTRODUCTION

"WHAT'S THE WORST THAT COULD HAPPEN?" My two brothers and I were riding an elevated train into Manhattan when we passed Silvercup Studios. At thirty-seven, I was the oldest brother and the one asking the question. Dan was three years younger than I was and an engineer living in San Francisco. Mike was an actor and film student in his early twenties and the only one of us living in New York. Mike was nervous about applying for a job at Silvercup. They hired crews for TV and film production in the spring. It was April. I told him to apply. I said, "Look at it this way. The worst they can do is say no."

"Unless they tell a fat-mama joke," said Dan. "They could say, 'Not only are we *not* going to hire you, but your mama is *so* fat...'"

o

Here is a frame.

Let's say that the frame represents the view of the scene you imagined after reading the first section of this introduction. Inside that frame are three brothers riding a train into Manhattan. I specified that it was an elevated train, but I didn't mention that from inside the train we could look down onto the roof of Silvercup Studios. You might have imagined the train at the bottom of that frame and the building rising up into the upper part of the frame. If you imagined yourself inside the train, you might have looked up at the rising facade of Silvercup Studios.

Even today I imagine the scene from my point of view back then. I was there and saw the view for myself. I looked out the train window and looked down onto the Silvercup roof and saw the big metal letters propped up and spelling out *Silvercup*. I fill that frame with what I remember of my experience, but I also fill that frame with my own imagination, influenced now by how I have described that scene in words. Any readers who had previously ridden that elevated train into Manhattan and seen Silvercup Studios would be familiar with the view. But now they too have to fill that frame with some of their own memories and mix in what they imagined after reading my written description. They might have ridden that train alone, but suddenly three brothers appear in the seats. One brother says, "Not only are we *not* going to hire you, but your mama is *so* fat..."

o

Here is a frame. It resembles the shape of a movie screen. And now you are seeing movies in your head. You are filling that screen with a movie you saw on a large theater screen, on a DVD player, on television, or even on your computer screen. I could have made a feature movie of the ride my brothers and I took on that elevated train into Manhattan. I could have made it the opening scene of a movie about a young man based on my brother Mike. This young man starts his new life in New York. He endures the advice and the razzing of his older brothers. Soon enough the young man must make his own way. That entire movie could be made to fit inside a rectangular frame.

I could also have made this into a short digital video and posted it on the internet. The scene could fit inside a frame of another shape, smaller, more square, but still containing three brothers inside an elevated train passing above Silvercup Studios on their way to Manhattan.

I could also have taken this scene and transformed it into part of a television commercial for, say, an online employment agency. The frame in which the commercial appears would depend on the frame of the television set. The frame might be rectangular, or it might have rounded edges.

I could have taken a photograph of the three of us on that train. I could have used a digital camera. The three of us would have leaned our heads together; I would have extended my arm to aim the camera back at us; my brothers would have made vulgar gestures; and I would have pressed the button. We could have seen ourselves moments later on the tiny screen on the back of the camera, a frame of about two inches wide and one and a half inches high.

That image could have been reproduced on many screens and filled frames of various sizes, from a computer screen to a print of eight inches by ten inches. If I had had the photo, I could have enlarged the image and mounted it on a billboard. But even without a photo, I could have painted a mural on a wall of a train station. I could have made a poster out of that scene. I could have made a postcard, a flyer, a holiday card. I could have written a novel and had an artist illustrate that scene for the book cover. There are lots of frames in the world. I could have filled any of them with that scene, with some version of three brothers riding an elevated train into Manhattan.

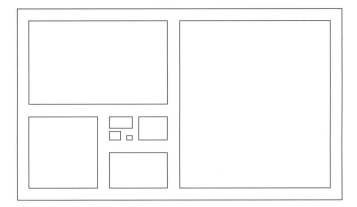

o

The scope of our vision is limited by our eyes. We see what we direct our eyes toward. The periphery of our frame of vision is blurred and indistinct. We move our eyes to shift our frame of vision. We turn our heads. The act of seeing depends a great deal on the muscles of the neck.

I wear glasses, which frame the world and bend the light of what I see, but I can see beyond the frames of my lenses. I can hold my fingers just in front of my chin and draw arcs with my left and right hands that circumscribe the limits of my frame of vision. I have done this exercise, and I feel as if I have traced the equivalent of a dog cone around my head. But that is a good analogy. The frame of my vision has an outer shape much like a cone. The cone is really two overlapping cones. The tips start at my eyes and enlarge voluminously out into the world.

In front of you is the frame of this sheet of paper, which happens to be six inches wide by nine inches high. I chose to fill this frame with words, which are themselves framed in a typeset column. These words have in turn created an imaginative frame in your mind. To be conscious of all this is part of what it means to be a graphic designer.

Yes, artists and ophthalmologists are also conscious of vision, and writers and readers appreciate the wonders of the imagination. But designers must be conscious of the act of seeing, of the limits of vision, and of frames—frames of perspective and frames of presentation.

o

I do a weird thing in my head when I think about designing something. I create a miniature world and fill it with people and objects. I might need buildings or mountains, clouds or fire. I can summon whatever I need in an instant. I set a hurricane into the palm of a banker's hand. I drop a plum into a bathtub of mercury. I flatten buildings and deal them like cards onto the green felt of a blackjack table. I am weightless and take up no space and can fly anywhere, outside a window or inside someone's ear canal. I am only a perspective, and I am hunting for the right view. There is a frame, and I am zipping around in this miniature world looking for the right perspective for this frame. I frame this way and that, tilting, warping, enlarging, and shrinking. From the street, I look up and a passing cloud changes into the sole of a shoe. From a cliff, I look down and a plummeting waterfall changes into the stream from a garden hose. The power of imagination is intoxicating. It doesn't feel like child's play. It feels like the play of a god.

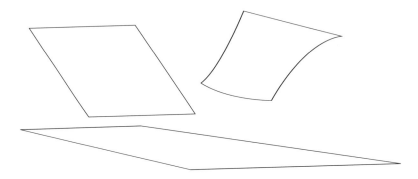

I wonder if past kings and queens enjoyed exercising their imaginations by enforcing rituals upon their subjects. Through ritual, we can organize the movements of others. We can frame our view of them. A courtier kneels before us. A lady curtsies. A general bows. A jester dances. The king and queen sit on elevated thrones and gaze down at the stage for the next ritual spectacle.

The powerful authorities of any time period continue to organize the movements of others. A political leader sends an army into battle. A company president sends employees to a new factory. A film director sends actors into the air on harnesses, suspended before a green screen on which is displayed the tanks and desert of a battle or the gears and machines of a factory. Those in control envision a frame for the action within a certain time and space—and especially a frame with the happy ending of a victory, a profit, a welcome myth, or all three.

A designer enjoys imaginative power more than political or economic power. Designers can do that weird thing in their heads. They can create miniature worlds. They can summon any person or object or natural phenomenon in an instant. They can re-create their imagined perspective within the boundaries of a frame in the real world. The frame can be made of paper or canvas. It can be a movie screen or a computer screen. Designers can frame the stillness of a Manhattan skyline or the movement of three brothers in an elevated train. They can give us a limited view of what they have been thinking about and looking at.

When I write about the work of other designers, I keep in mind all that goes into framing their views. Designers see, imagine, and create. It sounds simple. It isn't. We have to accept the limitations of our sight and the boundaries of our frames. We have to observe intently and frame our perspectives carefully and design our creations so that others may share our views. We are at our best not when we play like kings or gods but when we work like fellow inhabitants of a miraculous planet filled with an endless potential for new visions.

○

As a child, I sat in the doctor's waiting room and hunted for hidden pictures in *Highlights*-magazine illustrations. An outline of an owl hid in the leaves of a tree. A profile of a sailor appeared in the bricks of a house. Sick back at home, I reclined in a red beanbag chair and rubbed crayons over the mix-and-match templates from Mighty Men & Monster Maker (Tomy, 1978). Today I write about graphic design and design culture. I am still mixing and matching and looking for hidden meanings.

I have written enough about graphic design over the past five years to collect the material in this book. Prior to that, I had never written about graphic design. I went to law school but never practiced. Instead, I wrote short stories, a novel, and magazine articles.

I was hired in 1996 to write for Group 7500, a small Detroit company that provided print materials, graphic-design services, and exhibit installations for unions and auto companies. As a part-time employee, I took on additional duties for the sake of efficiency. I traveled, took pictures, and sketched layouts for the graphic designers. I asked the designer at that time, Donny Harder, to introduce me to the toolbar of PageMaker. After studying issues of *Print* magazine, I went to work. It was an illicit thrill. I was my own garage band.

In 2003, I read *Emigre* magazine for the first time. After reading issues 65 and 66, I was inspired to write about art, design, commerce, and consumerism. During three weeks in 2004, I wrote an autobiography of my own imagination. I submitted the manuscript to *Emigre*. Six months passed before editor Rudy VanderLans contacted me. *American Mutt Barks in the Yard* appeared in 2005 as *Emigre* 68.

Why I continue to write about graphic design is hard to explain. I hinted at my motivation in the earlier section on frames. I like graphic design, and I like it for many of the same reasons that I like to read and write books. Graphic design has the power to tell a story.

Writing and designing are, for me, solitary callings, and I answer when schedule permits. I am a dad, and I work at home. When daddy duty calls, I answer. So when I finally sit at my desk and work, I feel this as stolen time. The feeling recalls the illicit thrill of first learning graphic design as a wide-eyed amateur. I do not fit my family life into my work. I fit my work into my family life. It happens to be the balance my wife and I have struck.

I have found that there is only so much balance I can take before moody restlessness sets in. Herman Melville describes the condition on the first page of *Moby Dick* (1851). Melville writes in the voice of Ishmael: "Whenever I find myself growing grim about the mouth; whenever it is damp, drizzly November in my soul . . . it requires a strong moral principle to prevent me from deliberately stepping into the street, and methodically knocking people's hats off." Ishmael longed to escape society, board a ship, and set off for the open sea.

I just wrote a book.

o

This book has four sections. The first section consists of essays, articles, dialogues, and reviews. I often mix literary forms the way a child might sketch a superhero's torso and add a werewolf's legs.

The materials in the second section target the extreme expressions of self-help culture, especially the ways we try to redefine ourselves without doing any work. Making the materials for this section was wicked fun, pure and simple.

The third section is a hybrid of instruction, fiction, and aphorism. A short chapter explains the transition from the second section to this third section.

The fourth section contains extra material.

○

"Make it new." This was the Modernist slogan coined by poet Ezra Pound (1885–1972), who espoused new literary forms to earn the attention of people flocking to radio and film. In our age of webcams, blogs, online videos, and satellite TV, writers, designers, and artists must contend with even greater pressures to make it new. Design lives in two worlds, art and commerce, and its fertility as a subject will endure as long as its necessity as a practice endures. Commerce exerts its pressures on design to make it new (new products, inventions, efficiencies), and art finds ways to exert its pressures through experiments in exuberance, perspective, recklessness, and hard work. Design lives and breathes amphibiously in the oily waters of this tension.

The last lines of the preface to The Picture of Dorian Gray *(1891) by Oscar Wilde are: "We can forgive a man for making a useful thing as long as he does not admire it. The only excuse for making a useless thing is that one admires it intensely. All art is quite useless."*

Desire is a funny thing. It speaks in a language of aches and yearnings, and you respond with the activities of trial and error. You tread water in the middle of an ocean. If you don't want to sink and drown, you kick and swim. You bump into other swimmers. Waves wash over you. No swift current carries you downstream. You can't let go and hope for the best.

My brother Dan still runs his engineering firm in San Francisco. Mike waits tables in the West Village, acts in plays, and keeps close to the subculture he loves, waiting for his break. I am in North Carolina. We all grew up in Michigan, but we have been kicking and swimming in three separate directions until we are now in three distant states.

I write because I love to write, and I hope that designers create because they love it and can't help it and wouldn't do anything else. Who can predict where your work will take you? Compromise is inevitable. Failure is inevitable too but not a reason to quit—or else I would have quit long ago.

No, I keep writing about design. Of course, not everyone is going to like what I write. But, I mean, what's the worst they could say?

DESIGN IS A HUG
AT A DISTANCE

I

INSPIRATION

What I realize must have happened the night before
when I wake up in bed with my work, disheveled and
glowing and a little embarrassed

PAR$_x$ADISE

THE NAMES OF DRUGS ARE WEARILY FAMILIAR TO ME.
Because my wife is a doctor, our family has to duck and
dodge like targets in a shooting arcade to avoid being tagged
with the name of a drug that combats allergies or acid
reflux. Pop! Allegra on a baseball cap. Pop! Nexium on a golf
shirt. Pop! Lipitor on a fridge magnet. We're like a family
in a poorly run witness-protection program. The mob will
find us sooner or later, like they found our travel mugs and
our sticky notes.

Essay on drug names

At a recent medical conference, I confronted a serene
world of bright ripe health. Exhibit signs flickered with
strange names. Photos depicted smiling babies, charitable
teens, and active retirees. Printed materials gleamed like
afterlife brochures dispensed at Heaven's gates. And that
was it: paradise. These were the new names of paradise. If I
took their pills, would I, too, be able to see clearly, breathe
easily, and get it up when I'm ninety-three?

Paradise now has more names than the artist formerly
known as Puff Daddy. Drug names exude a shimmer of
authoritative reassurance. It's all Latin for "Trust me. You'll
feel beautiful." The namers of drugs indulge their delusions
of "brandeur" and rename the garden of Eden. But this
can't be any old paradise. The names have to suggest an
empowering, scientifically assured paradise. The operation
of the drug must appear reliably mechanistic, as simple as
a lever when compared with biochemistry. The obscurity of
the brand name is a proxy for chemical complexity, which
fosters the consumer's deference to the experts. And yet the
magic words that open the cave of wonders must be simple
enough for Ali Baba to pronounce phonetically.

Arrayed in the medicine cabinet of Adam and Eve are: Aeroset, Biaxin, Fosamax, Maxalt, Propecia, Aclovate, Tikosyn, Lexiva, Arixtra, Valtrex, and Exelon. The letter *A* is as popular as the head of the cheerleading squad, and the letter *X* shoulders far more than its share up the mountain of scientific grandiosity. And if one is good, then two are better: Vioxx, Hyzaar, Bexxar, Xanax.

Drug names connote both paradise and the means to get you there, like naming a highway after the city it takes you to. Some of the historical names of earthly, celestial, and literary paradise are: Eden, Dilmun, Utopia, Shambhala, Oz, Nirvana, Firdaus, Minoo, Pardis, Punt, Erewhon, Valhalla, Olympus, El Dorado, Tlalocan, Suruga, Atlantis, Avalon, Garothman, Wonderland, Xanadu, Janna. The English word *paradise* derives from the Old Persian word *pairidaeza*, meaning "park" or "garden." *Janna* is Arabic for "garden" and means "paradise" in the Koran. The Koran has eight different names for paradise. Pfizer has eighty.

To name your own dream drugs, add a scientific-sounding morpheme to some historical name of paradise. Nirvastra. Levox. Janaquin. Xanadrin. Or add a scientific name or paradise name to a word that connotes empowerment or superiority. Flextra. Elitra. Oztrim. Suprantis. Edominatra. Just make sure it doesn't sound like an element of the periodic table (Paradium, Utopium, Eldoradium) or vaguely dirty (Dixogyn, Testicra, Vulvox).

Draw inspiration from the props of paradise, like flowers (Lilex, Rositra), birds (Dovaquil, Canarida), and rays of light (Sunamax, Solanz). Dig up old mythologies to learn the names of past inhabitants. Pfizer has several brand names that sound like the names of Greek goddesses: Aricept, Ellence, Inspra, Lyrica. In your own linguistic laboratory, throw a party for the Greek goddesses and introduce them to the nerdy but charmingly promiscuous Mr. X: Athena = Athexa; Hera = Hexa; Demeter = Demextra; Hestia = Hexia; Enyo = Enyox; and Aphrodite = Axrodita.

Harvest morphemes from the fields of science, strength, and paradise, but be warned: not every harvest yields an appetizing meal. Some of Amgen's brand names (Epogen, Kepivance, Kineret, Neulasta, Sensipar) are like word scrambles in the Sunday paper. A selection of drug names from Abbot Labs reads like a spelling test for a young

You can't hoard made-up names. You can apply for trademark status when the mark is in "use in commerce" or when you have a good-faith intent to use the mark in the future. If you claim "intent to use," you have to sign a sworn statement. Marks no longer in use are retired from registration and made available to others. U.S. Patent and Trademark Office: www.uspto.gov

Klingon: Kaletra, Mavik, Tarka, Ultane, Zemplar. Novartis inexplicably green-lighted the brand name Cataflam (catastrophe + flamboyant?). As a judgment call, the decision itself is a cataflam. Other cataflams from Novartis include Simulect (simulated + intellect?) and Starlix (obvious porn name). My son and I occasionally invent names for imaginary Pokémon characters, and apparently so do the folks at GlaxoSmith-Kline: Cutivate, Flovent, Fortaz, Navelbine, and Digibind.

Pharmaceuticals are big business, so big (a $643 billion global market in 2006) that the entire branding industry could fit inside one of Big Pharm's metaphorical gel caps. You could easily consume all the information and statistics about the industry you wanted by using Google, another new name for both paradise and the road that gets you there. It goes without Googling, however, that paradise does not exist, no road leads to El Dorado, and Panacea is nothing more than the name of a pharmaceutical company in Maryland. The history of humanity's attempts to create Utopia is, after all, the history of cataflams.

IMS Health ("the world's leading provider of information solutions to the pharmaceutical and healthcare industries") reports the global pharmaceutical market grew 7 percent in 2006 to $643 billion. www.imshealth.com

CARNAGE FOR KIDS

MY KIDS AND I TOUR THE AISLES AT BLOCKBUSTER.
We look at the new releases, which occupy the shelves along
the outer wall. The outer wall flows from one end of the
store to the other, from the front window all the way around
to where the Game Rush section starts. While the interior
aisles organize movies by genre (action, comedy, drama,
family), the new-release walls include all genres. My kids
and I walk the new-release walls the way everyone does:
gawk, shuffle-shuffle, gawk, shuffle-shuffle. I call this the
eyeball creep or the zombie scan. I barely move my legs, but
my eyes are in overdrive. What sets us parents with kids
apart from, say, the teens on dates is that we vary our gawk-
shuffle-shuffle to include the quick-cover-your-eyes and
the bury-your-face-in-my-shoulder.

Essay on gory DVD covers

Horror movies.

The DVDs of horror movies are included with every other
genre of new-release DVDs on Blockbuster's walls. That
means *Andre the Butcher* chops next to *Aquamarine*. *Cello*
accompanies *Cheaper by the Dozen 2*. *The Descent* snuggles up
to *Dr. Doolittle 3*. *Harry Potter*, *Hoot*, *Hoodwinked*, and *How to
Eat Fried Worms* share real estate with *House of Blood*, *Heart
Stopper*, *Headspace*, *Haunted Highway*, and *The Hills Have Eyes
(Unrated)*. And, yes, these are the actual arrangements as I
saw them and wrote them down while I was in Blockbuster
scanning the walls for jarring juxtapositions.

I'm no censor. I just think it's common sense to separate
new releases by genre. If you separate nothing else, you'd
think it would at least make sense to separate the horror
movies from the kid titles. Bam. Problem solved.

*Rental DVDs shelved
together in 2007*

But Blockbuster doesn't, and it's been this way for as long as I've had kids. My kids are now ten and eleven. Even today I tell them to move quickly past *Machined* and *Maid of Honor, Pulse* and *Pumpkin Karver*. When my kids were younger, I'd just pick them up and have them look away or do the gawk-shuffle-shuffle with my hands covering my daughter's eyes. I never thought it good policy to leave the kids alone in the video-game section or the non-new-release kid section, but sometimes, yes, I did that. I was tall enough to look over the aisles and see them (gawk, kid check, shuffle-shuffle, gawk, kid check). The threat of Mr. Creepy Loner accosting my kids was rare and abstract, but the threat of *Mr. Hell* and *Mr. Jingles* scaring the shit out of my kids was pretty much right in our faces. Bam. And then it's welcome to three nights of nightmares on my street.

I've been thinking about this issue for years. I've never known quite what to say about it. It's one place where graphic design hits me emotionally—if not ambushes me—and has a real effect on my behavior. I realize that blame for creating the gory DVD covers should not be placed solely on the graphic-design teams. They surely had strict horror-movie criteria dictated to them by the film-industry marketers. I blame the marketers and the designers. They both should take credit where credit is gruesome.

For years I hoped Blockbuster would read my mind and separate genres. They haven't done that yet, but they have moved the kid new releases to an outer wall, a single shelving unit of *Bob the Builder* and *Thomas the Tank Engine* DVDs measured in a single gawk-shuffle-shuffle, and then it's back to the mélange of carnage and comedy, action and dismemberment. By the way, I'm not a prude. I'm disturbed by lacerated bodies, strung up and gutted, not naked ones, pumped up and thonged. I don't care for horror flicks, but I don't begrudge the tastes of horror fans. I'm all for the free-to half of our civil rights, but I'm also in favor of the free-from half. Others are free to watch *Silent Scream*. I'd like my kids to be free from seeing the cover for *Severed*.

I've often thought that the juxtaposition was on purpose. How much faster do I thoughtlessly grab the kid DVD when it's surrounded by slaughtered torsos? What else could explain my renting of the latest Tim Allen movie except that I wanted to protect my kids from seeing the covers for *Art of the Devil II* or *Satan's Little Helper?* "Have you guys seen *The Shaggy Dog?* No? Great. Let's get out of here."

I'd have less cause for complaint if the graphic designs of these DVD covers weren't becoming so graphic. Today's horror movies are about gore and torture, not fear and anxiety. Or maybe they're really about technology, using computer animation to tear people to shreds in some ironic foreshadowing of a future day when computers really do tear us to shreds. Today's horror movies are not subtle glosses on *Psycho*. *Psycho* is a public-service announcement compared to today's viscera porn. The covers represent this increasingly graphic and brutal trend. There's nothing suggestive. It's all literal. It's *Disembowelment for Dummies*. The covers show what the movies are about by showing more of the movie, and more of today's movies are about the equivalence between sushi and people. Your horror order is up: people sushi, with a chainsaw. And a meat hook. And a drill. And a blowtorch. And a needle and thread to sew the pieces back together and start all over again.

I could make a nuanced argument about how the DVD covers arrayed on Blockbuster's new-release wall reflect our dreams back to us, our hopes and fears given graphic literal expression in a microcosmic diorama of America's self-regard. I think, however, that this is bullshit. I might want to find accidental art in this gallery of gore, but what's on the shelves reveals nothing more than reckless marketing. No DVD-rental franchise is trying to make an artistic statement about the content of America's soul. They are—via the horror, the horror of graphic design—trying to make me switch to Netflix.

Schlock and maw

EVOLOGO

THE IMAGE IS A TROUBLEMAKER. Intended to simplify the difficult concept of evolution, the sequence of ape to hominid to *Homo sapiens* has come to stand for evolution itself. The graphic is more powerful than the concept, more moving than the caption, more seductive as a narrative myth of our beginnings than any three-hundred-page book by Richard Leakey or Stephen Jay Gould. It is also inaccurate, misunderstood, and misleading.

"The Time-Life book is the reason this image became so ubiquitous," says Professor F. Clark Howell, professor emeritus in anthropology at the University of California, Berkeley, referring to his incredibly popular Time-Life book, *Early Man*. First published by Time Books in 1966 and thereafter part of the Life Nature and Young Reader's Libraries, *Early Man* featured artist Rudy Zallinger's illustrations of our evolutionary forebears lined up as if on parade, beginning with a hunched, long-armed gibbon and ending with a rigidly upright modern man. Millions of copies were printed. "The artist didn't intend to reduce the evolution of man to a linear sequence," continues Howell, "but it was read that way by viewers." The text admits that, for comparison's sake, some of the early primates were drawn walking upright rather than on all fours, and later editions clarified that the progression was not a straight, smooth path. However, "the graphic overwhelmed the text," says Howell. "It was so powerful and emotional."

Rudy Zallinger (1919–1995) contributed greatly to the art of natural history. Depicting 350 million years of life in one epic sweep, his 110´ x 16´ mural Age of Reptiles *on the wall of Yale's Peabody Museum of Natural History earned him a 1949 Pulitzer Prize. Zallinger also made the 60´ x 5.5´ mural* Age of Mammals *in 1967 for the Peabody Musuem. In* Beasts of Eden *(2004), author David Rains Wallace includes this quote from Zallinger: "I ultimately proposed a different convention, that of using the entire available wall . . . for a 'panorama of time,' effecting a symbolic reference to the evolutionary history of the Earth's life." Zallinger remained the Peabody's artist-in-residence until his death.*

*Zallinger's famous
illustrations for the
wildly successful
Time-Life book*
Early Man (1968)

Hominid evolution proceeds in fits and starts, digressions and extinctions. For decades, textbooks have emphasized that *Homo sapiens, Homo erectus,* and *Homo neanderthalensis* quite possibly share a common ancestor *(Australopithecus anamensis),* but they did not evolve in orderly single file as if riding an escalator in a magazine cartoon. Naturalist Jay Matternes created art for a November 1985 issue of *National Geographic* in which the viewer looks hominids in the face as they emerge, scattered, from the foggy branches of prehistoric time.

More accurate graphics, however, seem to be no match for the original image. To this day, in movies and logos, cartoons and magazine covers, the legacy of Zallinger's *March of Progress,* as his graphic came to be called, persists in a reductivist form. An ape on the CD cover for the soundtrack to 1992's *Encino Man* evolves into a skateboarder. An inside-cover illustration for Richard Leakey's 1978 book *People of the Lake* shows a staggered crowd of apes, hominids, and people emerging from a forest, the art being notable for including females (most renditions presume that evolution can proceed just fine with a chorus line of males). The logo for the Leakey Foundation features a small silhouette of the image. In the March 3, 1994, issue of *Time* magazine, the graphic *Humanity's Long March* relies on the same tropes as Zallinger's image (a left-to-right sequence of apes to men) even as it includes a more complicated (though now outdated) graph beneath it. In a 1998 *Rolling Stone* feature, Ben Stiller evolves from a hairy ape to a naked actor. And in a December 2005 issue of the *Economist,* hominids lope up a flight of stairs and evolve into a woman in a black dress holding a glass of champagne.

The introduction of stairs reveals the underlying misinterpretation: that evolution equals advancement. Evolution operates without intent, without judgment. Species change over time, genes mutate, accidents happen. A comet hits. An ice age cometh. The science of evolution examines how life has changed and continues to change. Scientists resist value judgments overestimating the importance of humans. We aren't the end-all of evolution simply because we happen to be the sudden champions of the here and now. Cockroaches, fish, and ferns have been around a lot longer than we have,

Hominids are primates within the family Hominidae. *This includes* Homo habilis, Homo erectus, Homo neanderthalensis, *and the only surviving species,* Homo sapiens *(us). Descendants of the family* Australopithecus, *hominids have been around for over two million years. Some species existed at the same time. Others died out, leaving no direct descendants. Distinctions between species are made on a variety of factors, including skeletal structure, brain size, the ability to walk upright, the use of tools, etc. As the fossil record grows, scientists redefine the boundaries between species.*

One explanation for its popularity among cartoonists is that the image collapses twenty-five million years of human history into a progression no more complicated than dot, line, square. The image humiliates us as a species (and exposes our crude struggle to understand ourselves). Provoking laughter at our humiliations is what cartooning is all about.

*Clockwise from top:
album cover art for the
soundtrack to the 1992
movie* Encino Man;
*F. Clark Howell,
author of* Early Man,
in his office in 2006;
Rolling Stone *spreads
for a 1998 story on
Ben Stiller; cover of
the December 2005*
Economist

and Earth still has a few chapters of her memoir to write. Nevertheless, Zallinger's March of Progress has become, in the public's mind, a mark of our progress. It's an easy mistake to make, because it is such a self-congratulatory one. Human evolution becomes a kind of million-year publicity campaign for your own personal premiere on the stage of history. The apes and cavemen have come and gone until, finally, you the man! Evolution-as-progress seduces us, too, with the simplicity of its storyline. Science is complicated and demands study (and humility), but three apemen in a line? Hey, what's to know?

The image looks simple, but deciphering it demands several leaps of imagination. Each primate or hominid stands for an entire species as well as an era spanning, in some cases, millions of years. Each member of the line is a symbol, a placeholder for an idea. Moving from one symbolic biped to the next glosses over exactly what is so difficult for us to imagine: what real evolutionary transition looks like over time. Leaping from galloping monkey to hunching hominid to upright human teases us into thinking we can indeed see evolution at work: it's nothing more than a series of movie stills in which a monkey stands up, shaves himself, and walks offstage a dapper gentleman. Life is a short film with a hairy beginning, a monosyllabic middle, and a happy end.

Advertisers presume the public prefers the short, funny film of human progress to the long, neutral inquiries of science. In a 1998 four-page ad in the *New Yorker,* an ape evolves into Johnnie Walker: "Welcome to Civilization." In a late-1980s airline print ad, stooped travelers at baggage claim morph into the breezy bipeds who fly South African Airways; the tagline asks, "How evolved is your long haul airline?" In a 1991 Toshiba print ad, apes lugging old computers are transformed into a man toting a laptop; the copy explains that a desktop computer is "a lower form" and "isn't advanced enough."

Diane Gifford-Gonzalez, an anthropology professor at University of California, Santa Cruz, has wondered for years why advertisers presume the public will appreciate the message. "The image is read as a simplistic old-fashioned icon placed in a contemporary ironic context. The icon

We think, therefore we err. In vanity, we privilege ourselves as the pinnacle of evolution. In the December 2002 issue of Nature, *Senior Editor Henry Gee blames Ernst Haeckel for smuggling Germany's natural philosophy (humans are #1!) into scientific thinking about evolution. Gee writes, "[T]he progressive view resonates far more strongly with our own vanity and inclinations than with the more abstract and austere concept of evolution by mindless selection."*

Some mistakenly believe the image embodies the principles of evolutionary science itself, with the righteous critic attacking evolution for propounding a theory of clean linear progression. Critics have been misinterpreting the science in this way since Darwin's time, and what they criticize is not evolution but their own caricatures of it.

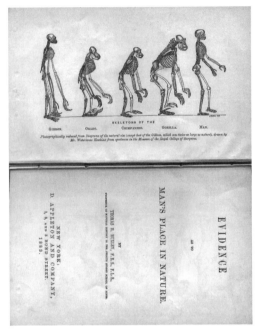

Clockwise from top left: frontispiece of Thomas H. Huxley's 1883 book Evidence as to Man's Place in Nature; Ernst Haeckel's 1874 illustration Ever Since Darwin reveals racist attitudes of early thinkers; illustration from Richard Leakey's 1978 book People of the Lake is notable for including women; the parody Man Is But a Worm appeared in an 1882 issue of Punch magazine

condenses history and then pairs it with a whiskey or airline or computer. The way ads use this image to represent human advancement suggests that their creators don't accept the story it tells as the literal truth, but rather as an icon to be played with."

Playing with parodies of evolution is not new. Artists first began spoofing the idea over one hundred years ago. The cartoon *Man Is But a Worm*, published in the 1882 issue of the British magazine *Punch*, shows a spiraling sequence of worms evolving into monkeys evolving into cavemen evolving into a British fop, with Darwin, robed and frowning, presiding at the center. Flash forward to Gary Larson's 1984 postmodern cartoon, *Evolution of the Stickman*, in which the cartooning art itself is lampooned as a stick snake gradually evolves into a stickman with a top hat and briefcase.

The icon of evolution descends from parodies and, even earlier, from comparison sketches. In the 1860s, Ernst Haeckel drew embryos to illustrate the evolutionary similarities among apes, pigs, and humans, but he distorted the renderings to bolster his argument. The frontispiece illustration for Thomas H. Huxley's 1883 book *Evidence as to Man's Place in Nature* reproduces the work of an earlier artist who had drawn the skeletons of a gibbon, orangutan, chimpanzee, gorilla, and human. For comparison's sake, Huxley reproduced the drawings out of scale, as if the subjects were all nearly the same height, and they are shown in single file from left to right. They are meant to depict not evolution but structural parallels.

In 1866, Haeckel was the first to use tree branches as a metaphorical technique for depicting relations among organisms, but his 1874 sketch of an African person sitting in a tree with monkeys reveals the racist attitudes of some early evolutionary thinkers (see Gould's 1981 book, *The Mismeasure of Man*). In 1867, a naturalist named Culver, a fan of evolution as then propounded by Huxley, drew the rather imaginative illustration *The Modern Theory of the Descent of Man* in which a dinosaur evolves into a platypus, and a kangaroo evolves into a person. Thankfully, Charles Darwin published *The Descent of Man* in 1871.

Adapted to fit every use, the graphic seems destined to survive and doomed to promote its fallacies. It encapsulates

*See Chris Mooney's
article "The Dover
Monkey Trial" in the
October/November
2005 issue of
Seed magazine.*

our human comedy as easily as it encourages misunder-standing of our human origins. A few years ago, a student at Dover Area High School in Pennsylvania painted a large artwork showing hominids, running in a field, that evolve into modern man. A janitor, lacking wit but not whim, took it outside and burned it.

THE MODERN THEORY OF THE DESCENT OF MAN.

*A naturalist named
Culver published the
fancifully misguided
illustration* Modern
Theory of the
Descent of Man *in 1867, four years
before Darwin's* The
Descent of Man.

MAN AND WIHF

"SHUT THE HELL UP!"

We are driving home from a weekend at the beach. I'm kneeing the wheel of the minivan while flipping for a new CD. In the passenger seat my wife concentrates on knitting a baby blanket (a gift) while habitually glancing at her pager. The kids are in back. Behind them, the dog curls up in the evening sun and chases squirrels in a Dramamine dream.

Shut the hell up?

Each child presides in a captain's chair. Deer Park water bottles slosh in the flip-out drink holders. Snack boxes erupt out of a shopping bag. The kids wear earphones or, as they call them, "earmuffs." On the portable Toshiba DVD player swaying in the hammock slung between the front seats plays *Shrek 2* or *Madagascar* or *Dinotopia*. The movie ends. The earmuffs come off and get hung on the straps of the DVD hammock. And then my daughter, eleven, makes one of her under-the-breath trademarked comments to my son, ten, who snaps, "Shut the hell up!"

My wife knits. Incredible. She doesn't even look up. Miraculous. She's waiting to see what I'll do. Because this, of course, is not my son's fault. It's mine.

My wife and I are working parents. She is a family doctor and I, as a friend once joked, am the doctor's wife. Nowadays, that's "WIHF." Before I'd read Ellen Lupton's recent essay, I hadn't heard that term. Working In Home Father. Or is it Working At Home Father, WAHF? No. Sounds too much like other WAFs: Women in the Air Force, the World Armwrestling Federation, the Workers Autonomous Federation, a Chinese union. Yes, I'm an exploited WWII

Essay on being a working parent

Ellen Lupton's essay "The Myth of the Working Mom" was published online at AIGA's Voice.

pilot armwrestling Chinese women. "Hold your grievances, boys. We've got a textile worker at two o'clock. Dive, dive!"

My mind flits like this, from light to light, as I stand and slice apples or sit and set type. I star in *Daddy Day Care* meets *The Shining*. This is the crazy that working parenting is. Take a WIHF.

I toss my son's soccer uniform into the washing machine, mix a batch of blueberry muffins, nuke a lunch of veggie nuggets, sketch next month's calendar on posterboard, check my daughter's math homework, and squeeze the dog's heartworm pill into a ball of cheddar cheese, all the while entertaining myself by mimicking Jim Carrey ("all rightey then") and Mrs. Doubtfire ("all right, dear") leading to Shrek ("no, you great stupid pastry") and then to Mr. Miyagi ("squish, like grape"). Lost in reverie, I detect the faint strains of familiar music, there, cutting through the nutty clutter of my mind, the sweet voice of my daughter, kindly wondering, "Maybe you need some alone time? Dad?"

No. I don't. I get a lot of alone time. Alone time is what I get. Ten years of it.

Let me rephrase. I have had alone time only since the kids started school. Prior to that, I had kid time. Actually, looking back, it's all so complicated. The balance of our lives changed year to year, if not day to day. There's no such preformatted family situation that dual-working parents set up once and then forget about. I wish I could go to Costco or Wal-Mart and buy a family setup like that, something like one of those party canopies you unzip and toss in the air and, by the time it hits, the thing has unfolded its legs and landed squarely on the bright green lawn of your expectations. But it doesn't work like that. Everyone struggles to achieve their own uniquely makeshift compromise of work and family. I am tempted to generalize from my own experience because that is what people, especially parents, do, abstracting their frustration in order to find solace in the shared plight of working parents the world over. I do it this way. You do it that way. Either way, the Man has us jumping, don't he?

Allow me to generalize. Today's dual-working-parent household survives like a desperate jazz band on a leaky ship, improvising riffs and solos as if the music powered the motors of salaries and bonuses, caulked the holes of credit-card debt, steered the course of college funds and

401(k)s. Whatever it takes: nannies, day care, part-time, flex-work, Daddy here, Mommy go, Mommy stay, Daddy back soon. In my case, our arrangement is not described by pert acronyms or phrases that include the word *sharing*. We live, instead, in apprehension of the instability of what is currently, if only barely, the case, and we are sustained by the hope that things will, someday, get better.

Ha.

The family as social bedrock has cracked under the stress of the job system, which has narrowed the needle of its efficiencies to fit into the groove of the individual, not the family. And so we, as individuals, are being played to generate music we do not have the ears to hear or the legs to dance to.

While I espouse the honor of pursuing one's calling, I am, by necessity, an e-serf on a celluleash. I am a mercenary money-grubber, an insistent perk-sniffer, apropos of the wildly unhinged employment relationships inherited (and accelerated) by my tech-addled generation (Ye Olde Generation X.O). My wife brings home the bacon, a third of which goes to Sallie Mae and the Department of Education, for we are indentured graduates (still) and half of which goes to the Bank of America, for we have a home mortgage (thanks to a boost from my Boomers-in-law). My wife, the beautiful wonderful generous family doctor for whom I do situps and pushups and drink lite beer, works late. I design magazines and books, but honestly that's the least of it. Mostly I wake the kids and feed them and drive them to kindergarten, first grade, second grade, third grade...fourth grade.....fifth grade...........sixth grade......... And after school, what's with the homework? We do rote penance at the kitchen table until dinner and even after that and then even in the morning. It's Groundhog Day. Where's Mommy? She's getting ready. She'll be home soon. She had to leave early. She'll be home late.

When we were twentysomethings living in an apartment, I stood in the tiny kitchen, Mac laptop on the countertop, mac and cheese on the stovetop, while interviewing lawyers for a legal magazine and aiming the remote control at the VHS of *The Lion King* so my two toddlers would continue to romp quietly on the bare mattress I'd thrown on the living-room floor in one of my what-the-hell's-the-difference moods. I was stranded on the island of my working-at-home apartment while my wife finished her fourth year of medical school.

Now, ten years later, I stand in our open-floor-plan kitchen, Dell desktop with wireless internet and 100 gigs of memory whirring in the home-office library, the latest recipe from *Cook's Illustrated* necessitating the warming of the outdoor grill, the plugging in of the KitchenAid mixer, the molding of mini–crab cakes. And while the kids beg for help with story problems and weather patterns and the definitions of *deign*, *plinth*, and *portico*, I listen to my mother on my wireless headset, click to call-waiting to hear my wife say she's still got an hour of dictating charts, switch back to my mom who's happy with the business cards I made her, and try to jot notes in a tiny Moleskine notebook for ideas about how I can make more money doing design and writing as a freelancer because I just lost my job.

It would be nice if work/family arrangements were as stable as gyroscopes, locking you in a saving embrace with the gravity of predictable days and the steady spin of candlelit nights. But nothing stays the same. Not even Daddy, Inc.

The day after my son growled, "Shut the hell up," revealing not only the limits of his self-control but the limits of my parental influence, I lost my job. It was the job I had had since the very day my son was born in 1996. I left my wife in the hospital to interview Health and Safety reps at a Michigan auto plant. I started as a writer for an in-house magazine, but soon I was traveling the Midwest, interviewing employees, photographing them on the line, art-directing the magazine, and acting as client liaison. I look back on these years with nostalgia now that I've lost my job. We had a nanny for the three years in which I traveled the most and designed the most and learned the most (and earned the most, enough to split my check with a nanny, aye, aargh, those were rum years for auto pirates, the SUV Nineties, the American industry's good years). When times got tough in 2000, and tougher in the years since, the magazine dwindled until now it is kaput. I don't pretend to know much about the situation the auto industries face. I just appreciate that for ten years my situation was damn good. I wasn't paid much in money, but I was rich with time.

I was a full-time at-home childrearing dad and a part-time home-office frequent-flyer-mile designer. I was the doctor's WIHF.

Now I'm unemployed, in debt, and facing about three hours of grade-school homework every night for the next eight years. My working life has cracked again, its tectonic plates floating away from the pristine supercontinent that was my part-time Pangaea (my daughter has a geography class, so sue me). Family, though, goes on. My kids are growing up. Their needs knock me around on the bumper car of my daily domestic existence. My wife sees patients at the office and sees the kids on nights and weekends. I email clients from my home office and care for the kids (providing meals, answers, dirty jokes, and mild insanity) for the seventeen hours a day the kids are not in school. In the dining room, my daughter sings, my son bangs the piano, I play the drums, and my wife shakes a tambourine while the dog chases its tail. The big bad economy will have its way with us, but that doesn't mean we have to go quietly.

DESIGNER SNAKES

A CINNAMON PASTEL SELLS FOR $1,000. A Pastel Ghost for $15,000. A Lavender Albino for $40,000. These are snakes, bred and interbred not for temperament or size or any quality other than beauty, which is skin deep and several feet long.

Beauty expressed in color and pattern. It's that simple. In the wild, snake skin varies according to chance mutations in offspring. In captivity, snakes are bred to create new colors and patterns. They're called designer morphs. They fetch high prices, initially, but both breeders and pet owners say they buy them for their beauty.

Essay on genetic design for beauty

Red Axanthic. Blonde Pastel. Lemon Blast. Peach Ghost. Orange Ghost. Butterscotch Ghost. Caramel Albino. Yellow Belly. Snowball. Banana. Pastel Jungle. Lesser Platinum. Mojave. Calico. Sable. Pewter. Goblin. Clown. Bumblebee. Killerbee. Piebald. Pinstripe.

These names do not refer to Pantone colors, paper stocks, fabric patterns, paint swatches, ice-cream flavors, or mixed drinks. They are the names of ball-python morphs. Ball pythons are popular because they're calm, slow, rarely bite, and remain small, less than six feet in length. They eat mice and rats. One two-foot female inhabits a terrarium on my son's desk.

As a kid I caught garter snakes in tall weeds. I kept them for years, but when one had nineteen live babies, I released them all in a nature preserve. I wanted an Indigo snake, large, aggressive, and gorgeous, and I read a few books on them. But my fascination ended quickly. My son, however, has the power of the internet, and at ten years old, he knows enough to host his own reptile show on Nickelodeon.

A young Piebald ball python on sale from TBM Constrictors

Spider, Lesser Platinum, and Pastel ball pythons on sale from VMW Reptiles

Cases display ball-python morphs for sale. All photos were taken on August 30, 2008, at the Carolina Reptile and Exotic Animal Show held on the North Carolina State Fairgrounds in Raleigh.

He wanted a snake. Badly. "Let's do the research," I stalled. Dozens of books and hundreds of websites are devoted to snakes, especially ball pythons. My son spent as many hours staring at python pics as he used to spend staring at Pokémon characters, and the comparison of the two is worth noting. Pokémon characters are endlessly varied, they "evolve," and new characters come out every other day. Same with ball pythons. There are hundreds of morphs, the morphs are bred to make more morphs, and new morphs arrive on the market every year. My son bought countless Pokémon magazines. Now he buys reptile and snake magazines.

Curiosity. Variety. Obsession.

My son bought his ball python at a reptile show in Raleigh, North Carolina. Several hundred people attended the show. I was amazed. The people who buy snakes for pets run the gamut, but the people who breed and sell them are all business. This is a serious subculture of people who truly love snakes. They appreciate their beauty. They spend money, time, and occasionally their working lives on them. Meanwhile, we named our snake Miracle because it was a miracle my wife let it into the house.

Albino snakes lack dark colors; axanthic lack yellow; and hypomelanistic, the "ghost" pythons, have less melanin than normal. Breeders get deep into the genetics of crossing morphs. The Pewter morph, for example, is a cross of a Cinnamon Pastel and a Pastel Jungle. The Piebald python looks like a regular python in a ripped white tube sock.

See ballpythonmorphs.com.

Designers could, of course, re-create python patterns on curtains and sneakers, pillows and handbags, ties, belts, socks, and scarves. A type designer could create a snakeskin glyph set called Slitherer. Beauty can inspire, and it can be reproduced. But I'm more fascinated by the process of morphing itself: the design of living things for beauty.

Snake design depends on genetics, mating parents of different genotypes to produce offspring with various phenotypes, some predictably patterned, others surprisingly so. Over the centuries, dogs have been bred for utility; dog breeds are like tools in a Swiss Army knife, a dog for every job. Ball pythons aren't bred for utility. They don't do anything but eat and grow. They're bred for their looks, and they're bred experimentally. Who knows what they'll look like? Just keep mixing them up. They're more like mutts. Mutts are accidents, beyond human influence. Python morphs are designed, by people, to look good.

Designer snakes set off associations. The synthetic snake in the movie *Blade Runner* (1982) was a kind of robot. The cows, sheep, and shark suspended in glass aquariums of formaldehyde by the artist Damien Hirst are fetish art, dead things that resonate with meaning. Artist Xiao Yu grafted the head of a human fetus (with the eyes of a rabbit) onto a bird as "a way for them to have another life." Figuratively, of course. Literally, these are dead things, body parts stuck together like a mythological creature.

Which brings us to the question: what is beautiful? Aside from the ethics of eugenics and corpse art, the search for new beauty drives people to crossbreed pythons for their skin patterns as much as it drives designers to experiment with line and color. Designs can be reproduced or mutated. So can snakes. Value derives from the investment of effort, the rarity of an outcome, the thrill of accident. And there is the living body, wherein lie natural resources to be mapped, harvested, and sold. Beauty is both a business and an obsession.

Appreciating the living beauty of a python moves people to buy it, to own it—like property, like art. The satisfaction of ownership leads to more buying and possibly to the start of a collection to sustain the high of owning beauty. *Gotta catch 'em all!* My son, naturally, wants another ball python. He's always hunting morphs online.

The thing about morphing familiar beauty into unfamiliar beauty is that the surprise of the new wears off. Soon, the mutant Cinnamon Pastel is as conventional as a normal ball python. And so you cross a Cinnamon with a Jungle to get your Pewter. The Cinnamon has descended from beautiful to useful. Beauty is what you plead when you're caught liking something too much. Utility is what's left when you've fallen out of love.

FOREVER SKULL

THE SKULL. The immortal icon of mortality. Overused, overexposed, overdone, and yet evergreen, everlasting, ever in play.

As an icon, it will never die, not as long as we are flesh and bone. We might one day become cyborgs, but the skull as symbol will morph into something like a drive-in-theater speaker, a metallic encasement with antennae and a mesh mouth. From primate to hominid to *Homo sapiens* to...roboskull. The skull will outlive us.

Between you and me, literally, the computer monitor is an exoskull. Like an insect's exoskeleton, the hardware houses the software. Welcome. The eyes (iEyes?) are the Windows to the soul.

We are not exoskeletal. We will never see our own skulls. And yet our brains reside within this bonehouse, like our hearts inside our ribcages. We are locked inside our skulls, these rooms of perception, never to leave them. We rarely see actual human skulls, but we constantly confront depictions, from the sequinned skull on a black Victoria's Secret bikini to a graphic rendering on the cover of the *New York Times Book Review* (for the 2007 book *Atomic Bazaar* by William Langewiesche). Empty-eyed on t-shirts and skateboards, grinning on black bandannas, flaming on the fuel tanks of Harleys, the skull is first a warning and then a boast. "Death comes to all," it warns. And in reply the boast: "I dare you."

See also the red skulls and crossbones decorating the bottles of Armida Winery's Poizin wine, packaged in little wooden coffins.

Death is forever. Skulls are forever. Diamonds are forever. And now, thanks to artist Damien Hirst, $100 million diamond death-skulls are forever. "Death comes to all," says this eight-thousand-gem-encrusted fake skull. "And it's shiny, like irony."

Death comes to all, like a gift you never need to deserve. Montezuma gave to Cortés a skull inlaid with turquoise, jet, and seashell: a symbol of death. Cortés, in return, gave death itself.

The symbol depends on the referent, the thing made of bone. And not just the skull but our ability to perceive it, to interpret it, to be conscious of what the skull might shake loose in our minds. The thing we see can't be our own skull: knock knock (dull thuds). It has to be another's skull, a dead person's skull, the empty melon, the cranial carapace: knock knock (cavernous echo). We see a symbol of ourselves that asks us to see ourselves. And so to see a real skull—clung with rot and soil, scraped, eroded, hair-clumped—to see this room deserted, it is a shock to the senses, an affront to our existence. No one lives there anymore. No one ever will.

I will never see my own skull, but my grandfather wanted me to imagine it, vividly. His warnings were so penetrating that they entered my mind when I was first learning to ride a bike and have resounded, thirty years later, out of my own mouth as I teach my son to ride a bike: "Be careful you don't crack your skull open." Then and now, I see the impact and the aftermath, the descent and the blood blooming across the sidewalk. In the shade of trees are the scattered acorns, the broken concrete, the canyon of cracked bone.

We will never see our own skulls. To be so close and yet so far. To see yourself alive for so short a time and never to see yourself dead, a state you will be in for so much longer. "Hi. It's nice to meet you." Blink. "I'm a skull."

This is what makes the skull so potent a symbol. All the ways we think about life and death, time and consciousness. On crucifixes, a skull and crossbones refer to the site of the crucifixion, Golgotha, "the place of a skull." Skulls for centuries marked the entrances to Spanish cemeteries. The first Royal Navy vessel to return from the war in Iraq in 2003 flew a Jolly Roger flag. The Seventeenth Lancers of the British Army adopted the skull and crossbones insignia in 1759. The U.S. Marine Corps reconnaissance battalions use the emblem. We use the symbol for spiritual reasons and for secular ones, in peacetime and in war. Pacifists use the skull as warning: death is the cost of ignoring reality. Warriors use the skull as boast: death is the cost of ignoring me.

Samples of Jolly Roger flags may be found at the website of the National Royal Navy Museum: www.rnsubmus.co.uk/ photodp/jrships.htm

The skull invites meditation on the locus of meditation. Forget Yorick. Picture a Chuck Jones cartoon. Our flesh is a suit out of which steps our skeleton. The suit of flesh sags to the floor, a puddle. But the skeleton somehow...moves. Without muscles, without flesh, it moves and it lives. Beyond that, it dances, all joints and angles and negative spaces, it dances a click-clackety jig. Ha ha ha. The Day of the Dead. But it's not us, not at all. And it's not our day.

Will we ever see consciousness, make thinking visible, like the eye seeing itself see itself? Not even our abstractions are this limber. The skull is the next best thing, a stand-in for the brain, the precious brain! To see a skull is to see the absence of the brain. Quoth the raven: "Never mind."

First published in 1845, the poem "The Raven" by Edgar Allen Poe features the refrain, "Quoth the raven, 'Nevermore.'"

Plastinated corpses: more stand-ins, more substitutes. A nearby museum features the Body Worlds show. Plastic-injected cadavers, skinless and as stiff-limbed as dolls, are worked into positions of suspended activity: midleap, midstride, but verifiably postlife. Still, this is just the bitter meat of our species. It's not me. It's someone else, or the paused rerun of a vivisected someone else. An "it."

We want to see ourselves stripped to the mechanistic dynamo, the soul in motion, the mind at work. Our desperate desire drives us to derivatives: the skull, the overuse of the skull, slapped across our cultural walls like plastic stars glowing in the dark. We're inured to them. It's too bright out for the skulls to glow, these faded blobs drifting farther and farther from the things they represent. We see skulls and think: poison, danger, pirate, X-ray, no diving, wear a helmet, midlife crisis ahead.

For more on skull decoration, see: socks, umbrellas, panties, toilet brush. Compare skull stacks and skull walls: Mayan rituals, American bison, Native Americans, the Holocaust, Cambodia. See also: German soldiers simulate oral sex with a skull plucked from a mass grave near Kabul, Afghanistan, for a photograph in 2006. Also in 2006, Wal-Mart sells t-shirts with the same skull symbol used by the Third SS Division, a unit of Adolf Hitler's Waffen-SS.

You mean symbols have histories?

The skull is an elastic symbol, but it expresses a frustrated desire: we will never see our own skulls. The impossibility of this self-knowledge maddens and tempts us. So we flatten our skulls, misshape them, adorn and prettify them, wrap them in thorns and set them afire, make them scary, funny, silly, slick, put them everywhere, on everything, for whatever excuse comes to mind. On and on, we are doomed to representations, teasing ourselves with reminders of the limits of our perceptions. We will never see our own skulls. But we will always want to.

Clockwise from top: HMS Unruffled's Jolly Roger (1941–1945) courtesy of the Royal Navy Submarine Museum, Gosport, Hampshire, UK; the death's head symbol used by a division of Hitler's Waffen-SS on the cover of the book SS-Totenkopf: The History of the "Death's Head" Division 1940–45 *(2001) by Chris Mann; comparison of Nazi death's head with photo of a t-shirt sold at Wal-mart, left, courtesy of Rick Rottman*

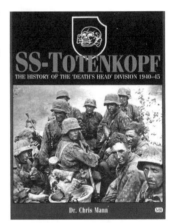

DESIRE'S DESIGN

Q: WHAT DO YOU WANT?

A: I don't know.

The dilemma of humanity encapsulated in a single Q and A. We don't know what we want. We don't know how to want. We don't know ourselves.

An essay on desire and consumption

Q: What do you want?

A: I don't know.

Among adults the exchange is like something out of a Samuel Beckett play. The question is asked again and again; the answer, always the same.

Q: What do you want?

A: I don't know.

I ask my kids a variation of this question a dozen times a day. What do you want to do? *I don't know.* What do you want to eat? *I don't know.* Where do you want to go? Who do you want to see? What is it that you want? *I don't know. I don't know. I don't know.*

If you don't know, who knows?

If you don't want, who wants?

Desire is not simple, singular, uniform among all people, homogenous within all minds. It's not a candy-bar emotion dispensed by the vending machine of the brain. If it were, if our desires were of the same nature and intensity, allowing for variation in the objects of our desire, then we would act on our desires exactly the same way every day. Every person would be engaged with the same enthusiasm, drive, and energy in activities as various as boxing and sweeping the sidewalk, cutting hair and driving a racecar, pole-vaulting and pumping gas. A standardized, one-size-fits-all desire would create a nightmarish world of automatons.

Instead, desire (as opposed to whim, caprice, lust, or appetite) can be understood as analogous to the clay of your identity, the seed of your personality. Or maybe not so literal or objective as clay or seed. Maybe something more ephemeral, insubstantial, subjective: a whisper, a shadow, a glimmer.

Acting on desire is more like a craft, a science, an art. It takes careful, mindful practice. Be patient and quiet. Listen, observe, take notes. Figure out what you want, privately, and then choose to want it, publicly. Put your desire out in the open. *I want to go swimming. I want to bake bread. I want to paint a picture. I want to build a chair. I want to write a book.* You act, and then you fail. Over and over. And it's better to start failing when you're young, when all you lose is an ice-cream cone or a baseball game or an afternoon of fun. When you're older, the stakes are higher. If adults don't know how to want, then they lose a love, a career, a life.

This is not an exercise in abstraction. People break down over this. They lose it. They go nuts. After her divorce, a woman goes shopping, a salesclerk asks her if there's anything she wants, and suddenly the woman weeps in the cereal aisle. People avoid high-school reunions because they don't want to admit they still don't know what they're doing. A guy retires and hangs around the house in a fog because he can't for the life of him remember what he retired *for*. In my home state of Michigan, unemployment is at 7.2 percent. A wartime recession tends to make folks moody and introspective. They wonder what the hell they're going to do.

Michigan Labor Market Information for February 2008, at Milmi.org

Q: What do you want?

A: I don't know.

The question doesn't care about good times or bad. It keeps coming at you.

Q: What do you want?

A: I don't know.

See Guns, Germs, and Steel, *the 1999 book by Jared Diamond, and* The Eternal Frontier, *a 2001 history of North America and its peoples by Tim Flannery.*

The exchange might describe the dilemma of any representative hominid over the last thirteen thousand years of our self-conscious existence. We have our primitive needs, yes: our needs for food, shelter, clothing, kinship, affection. But we are not hunter-gatherers anymore. We are not farmers in a feudal system. We are consumer-traders. Yet when our survival is no longer at stake, we still balk at defining our desires and, instead, substitute our primitive needs, the fulfillments of which are no longer primitive, no longer basic, no longer about survival. What do you want? *I don't know, but how about weapons and wealth, conquest and concubines, slaves and sugar? I don't know, but how about a hamburger and a hydrogen bomb, a cool drink and a new frontier?* The substitutions are temporary because the need to substitute remains. Why? Because the question has not been answered, only deferred.

Q: What do you want?

A: I don't know.

The deferment of desire drives our consumption of substitutes. We crave new meals, new movies, new machines. The American belief that there will always be more to consume derives from our frontier history—an economy of endless progress, the value of capital dependent on accelerating consumption. In the past couple hundred years (a simple inhalation of breath as measured by the lungs of time), U.S. progress depended on the bounty of North America's resources: land, fur, bison, tobacco, cotton, lumber, coal, corn, cattle, oil, steel, gas, lakes, and rivers. The waves of our progress swept up Native Americans and slaves and deposited railroads and cities. And now, of course, we have a globally interconnected economy of services and information, technology and finance.

Consumer spending accounts for 70 percent of U.S. gross domestic product. The U.S. economy depends on consumption, and we do a great deal of consuming while sitting on our lazy butts. There are 300 million of us, and we now spend as much money in restaurants as we do in grocery stores. We spend over $500 million on online dating services and personal ads, $3 billion on internet pornography, $16 billion on video games, $43 billion on movies, and $175 billion on online shopping. We like to consume so much that we overextend ourselves. U.S. credit-card debt is $790 billion (U.S. federal debt is $9.4 trillion), and while we're shopping online, we're losing our homes. The nation had foreclosure filings on 223,651 properties during the month of February 2008, a nearly 60 percent increase from February 2007.

Consumption is so much a part of who we believe we are that we can't control ourselves, even when pursuing it threatens our survival.

Sources: Consumer spending from U.S. Bureau of Economic Analysis / Restaurant spending from Economic Research Service, U.S. Department of Agriculture / Dating information from study by Online Publishers Association and comScore Networks / Internet-pornography revenue estimate from TopTenREVIEWS as well as Good Magazine / Video-games statistics from Consumer Electronics Association / Movie revenue estimate from Motion Picture Association / Online-shopping statistics from Forrester Research / Credit-card debt from Center for American Progress / Federal debt from U.S. National Debt Clock / Foreclosures from RealtyTrac's February 2008 U.S. Foreclosure Report

Q: What do you want?

A: I don't know.

I screwed up when I was younger. I had bad habits. I made self-defeating choices. I look back on my judgments, and I shake my head in wonder and shame. How could I be so ignorant of my own desires? I *wanted*, but I wasn't good at the *practice* of wanting. They're two separate things.

So, big me that I am, I'm pretending I know something about life, and I'm teaching my kids how to make choices. I don't know what I was expecting, but it's so much harder than I thought. Kids learn all the time, of course. They learn geometry and the culture of school, software programs and the rules of soccer. But they are not explicitly taught about desire, choice, and judgment. I always thought this was a real oversight, but now with my own kids, I can understand the omission. The quickest way to throw a roomful of kids into pandemonium is to ask them what they want. Kids have no desire and unlimited energy. It's a volatile combination.

Kids are a tough crowd: bored, frustrated, moody. So I've tried Reward and Punishment. *Try this, or else!* I've tried Warning and Invitation. *You're going to waste the day, so what do you think of giving this a try?* I explain the philosophy behind why I'm so insistent that they learn to make their own decisions. What happens? Apathy. Inertia. They push me into a corner. I have to do Limitation and Enforcement. No more choices. I'm the Decider. I force them to do what I want.

Q: What do you want?

A: I don't know.

Q: I do know. You want to do *this*.

A: No, I don't.

Q: You have to. Do it.

A: I hate you.

But they do it. And later, after playing basketball in the driveway or working in the yard or gluing a collage of magazine cutouts, they say it was fun. What a lesson! I haven't taught them to think about what they really want and make a choice. I've taught them to defer to authority. It's too much work to listen, observe, and summon desire from within the well of oneself. Instead, when asked what you want, you should just say, "I don't know. Tell me."

Brilliant.

Now I have a new tactic. I keep verbally hounding them about the importance of choice and the costs of default choices, like watching TV or YouTube. My son will do that and then after a couple hours complain that we didn't do anything fun. (There it is in action: distractions that defer the choice but are themselves the choice! There are no do-overs. You don't get the time back.) I take that moment to remind him of the consequences of his own choices (pain, the great educator and maker of angry sons), but I'm now trying to redefine my role as Introducer. I introduce them to the world of art and music, nature and exercise, cooking and yoga. This sounds so granola god awful as I write it that I have to beg your leave to explain. We sew, but we are inspired by *Project Runway*. We throw the football, but we mimic Brett Favre. We sing, but we're singing to a Liz Phair song. Pop culture is in our house, no question. But so are sarcasm, wit, and other self-defensive moves of our intellectual jujitsu.

The designer desires to create, and the creation operates as a means of communication—visual, verbal, or otherwise. The design itself may elicit curiosity. Or else the design just has to get in the way. That's me. I'm a parent. It's my job to get in the way. To design is to plan, and what is parenting if not a completely bewildering improvisation? We have a million moves available to us, and we can juke and jive until we find one that works.

Q: What do you want?

A: I don't know.

"This will do." That's what Kenya Hara says in his monograph *Designing Design* (2007). "We want to give customers the kind of satisfaction that comes out as, 'This will do,' not, 'This is what I want.' It's not appetite, but acceptance." He's talking about his design work for MUJI, and he explains that he designs with the recognition that Japan is a mature economy of limited resources. Japan is a consumer economy, but as an island, as an advanced culture, it does not subscribe to the myth of the unlimited frontier. They have to design wisely, generate value globally, and consume reasonably.

On the big island of North America, we're using up a lot of stuff. We're making a mess. We know it, and we've given our guilt a color: green.

We are aware, more than ever, of the consequences of our habits of consumption. We are mindful of our natural resources, of the scale of our appetite and our mess, of the cycle of our use from oil spill to landfill. As a culture and an economy, we are finally asking ourselves the question point blank.

Q: What do you want?

And because we haven't quite defined the terms yet, we produce the same answer.

A: I don't know.

A mature economy, seeing the desert of a wasteland on the horizon, is forced to restrict rates of consumption. People calm down, accept limits, and say, "This will do." But do for what? For the stuff we need, for the energy we use, for establishing the latest threshold of what passes for "survival" within our class. For satisfying our cravings for aesthetics and function, pleasure and appreciation. For satisfying our need to communicate and connect. Yes. And then what? What about our consumption is indeed sufficient to... do what again exactly?

To do what you want to do. To pursue your desire. The clay, the seed, the glimmer.

Please survive. And enjoy. Luxuriate even. (Says the mature economy.) Do not deprive yourself, sacrifice your liberty, or attack your way of life. Ask, instead, a much, much harder question. Go to the heart of the matter. Confront humanity's age-old dilemma. Ask the question planted within our primitive consciousness, the one each of us must ask of ourselves and answer with the remainders of our lives.

Q: What do you want?

A:

KENYA HARA

KENYA HARA SETS HIS BOLD IDEAS IN A COOL LAND-
SCAPE, LIKE CANDLES IN SNOW. *Designing Design*, at 470
pages, is as white as a prayer book and heavy as a dictionary.
It is a hybrid of monograph and forum for Hara's essays,
which often use his work and the work of others as case
studies. As designer, essayist, and exhibit curator, Hara
explores a revaluation of values in design, culture, and consumerism. The book is a wonder, but less for Hara's design
work and more for his design writing.

*Review of the designer's
2007 book* Designing
Design

Which is to say that his ideas hold far more potential to
influence designers than his physical works. To make this
point, Hara opens the book with over one hundred pages
devoted to the work of other designers (work showcased in
Hara's RE-DESIGN exhibition of redesigned daily objects,
such as toilet-paper rolls, tea bags, and matchsticks). The
book itself is evidence that Hara's work cannot be separated
from his writing. His designs flow from his imagination
and, in turn, feed his imagination. "Verbalizing design is
another act of design," he writes on the first page, and in
this bold and beautiful book, he proves it.

His biography appears on page 467 (award-winning
Japanese designer, born 1958; representative, Nippon
Design Center; professor, Musashino University), and his
own work does not appear until page 122. But don't mistake
this for humility. The book recruits four acolytes, Li Edelkoot,
John Maeda, Jasper Morrison, and Naoto Fukasawa, to praise
Hara as philosopher king, design guru, and prophet. The
publisher must have insisted on these overheated odes.
Ignore them, and remove the awkward half wrapper and
sticky dust jacket.

Cover and interior spreads reproduced by permission of the publisher from Kenya Hara, Designing Design *(Baden, Switzerland: Lars Müller Publishers, 2007)*

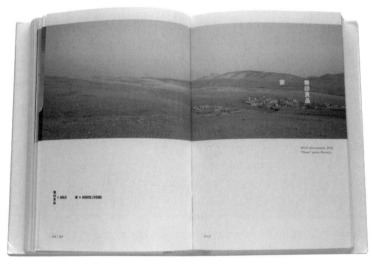

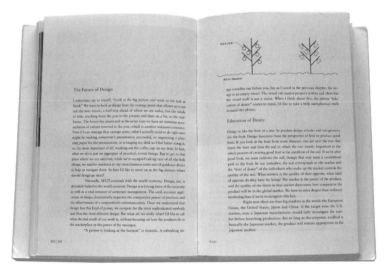

The fabric of the hardcover, in contrast to the dust jacket, feels intimate, even smudging during handling. Tactility is one of Hara's design concepts. In the chapter "Haptic," which relates to touch, Hara presents the work of other designers who redesigned objects, like tadpole coasters, gel doorknobs, and juice boxes covered with simulated fruit skins, soft and seedy. In the chapter "Senseware," Hara invites designers to consider touch, sound, and even memory as they search for new dimensions in their work. He presents his own designs—signage for hospitals and galleries, books for corporate clients and the Nagano Winter Olympics—not as models but as attempts in this direction.

Design for senses other than sight. For a literary exploration of a "haptograph," see the recent short story "The Wizard of West Orange" by Steven Millhauser, included in his book Dangerous Laughter *(2008).*

Hara moves from the small world of daily objects, the miracle of paper, and the meaning of white, to breathtaking panoramas of broad horizons (the MUJI advertising campaign), Japan's unique perspective on Western culture and commerce, and his intellectually rigorous proposal (rejected) for the World Exposition 2005 held in Japan. For MUJI, Hara counters the reckless exuberance of Western consumerism with the restraint of a mature economy, prompting people to say not, "I want this," but, rather, "This will do."

A truly radical concept for Americans

Hara values simplicity, sincerity, and respect for the complexity of humanity's relationship to the natural world. His values offer an alternative to the youth-obsessed and sex-crazy values of Western capitalism. Where does design go from here? Hara offers a view.

BOOK BOTHER

A BOOK IS AS COMMON AS A CEMETERY, BUT IT IS A PLACE WHERE WE BURY OUR DREAMS WITH MORE CEREMONY THAN SADNESS.

The first two books I ever made were *The Time Machine* and *Hell House*. I folded paper and stapled it at the spine. I glued end papers to cardboard covered in red fabric. I wrote the stories and drew the pictures. I made *Time* in fourth grade. I made *Hell* in fifth.

Twenty-four years later, I was doing the same thing for a chapbook of my short fiction. Computer, printer, and now digital press: these are tools I use to make books. Without these tools, I'd just use other tools: pen and paper, sidewalk and chalk, my head and the nearest wall.

I have used Xlibris, Booksurge, and Lulu to bury my dreams. I can only recommend print-on-demand as an expensive learning experience and not as a business proposition. You will lose a little of your innocence and a lot of your money.

Instead, make books using computers and bind them by hand. Sell your books person to person and online through websites and via Powell's or Amazon but rarely on consignment with bookstores (the transaction costs are too high). Use short-run digital presses when working with a small publisher to get your books into print economically and at high quality.

Behold your book and ask yourself, "Why, why, why?"

Why make a book? Why bother?

Making a book is a journey in which you go out into the world to find out what scares you the most, even if it's still yourself.

Making a book creates a midnight in which synaptic lightning illuminates our skull's planetarium. It lets us peek into how we think we might work. Our mind is the one organ that must envision both its own reflection and the mirror in which to see it.

One night, brushing my teeth and thinking about a book I'd just read, I examined my face in the mirror. There is something to be said about these private moments in which self-consciousness so proudly surveys its factory and savors the glory of its operation. Making a book is another means to savor that glory.

Bookmakers must peak in their thirties, because that's when you have achieved a perfect balance of experience and recklessness. You have lived through enough to have developed a perspective on the world, and you are young enough to believe your perspective matters.

Stone tablets.
Ones and zeros.

The last bookmaker has not yet been born. We have been burying our dreams for centuries. We will die. But books never will. We will always need cemeteries.

Why this solitary work? Fear. Possessiveness. The dumb bald nature of the beast of work. Selfishness, of a productive kind. We are terrified by the ignorance of our creation, and so we love with self-pity our own creations. This book here; I know who made it.

The written form of a book doesn't represent the form in which I believe life is lived or consciousness experienced. The written form only honors the form in which the thoughts come. A book is the delivery system for a hallucinogen you ingest through the eyes and digest in the mind. A book allows one imagination to taste the inside of another.

To create the content of a book—its text and images—is to lurch and stall, peak and burrow. Midwifing the physical book's production is another process toward satisfying the creative madness. To put the book out there, into the hands of others, is to surrender to a climax, and to a little death.

A reader's common complaint about a particular book is that it is not another book. Wishing for another book is wishing for one's own book. Or, more accurately, for the representation of one's own eccentric dream.

What is the point of delighting in the making of books when the delight fades so quickly, the curiosity dulls, the young grow old, and death gives us appetizers to its main course by erasing our memories here and there?

Books preserve. They memorialize, like an extra dry lobe of your brain, a sequential neural spill. Like a plaster cast of your neural footprint. The traced shadow of your mind.

Books comfort the young and healthy. Others have come and gone, leaving books behind, which reassure me that my mind is still strong, my heart is still beating, and I am not alone. But when I am old, stumbling, and grumpy, what illusion of solace will be left for me? Immortality through art? If I can't remember my own name, what do I care if others do?

Because the making makes the maker. You were not a bookmaker until you made a book. You moved, and you were moved. "And let's not forget," the book says, "that we existed."

At least not yet, not just now.

PAPERBACK FIGHTER

ASSEMBLING THE CONTENTS OF A BOOK IS LIKE
CURATING A ZOO. Experience is caged and put on display
and told to just act natural.

It's irresistable, this pull to make books.

Curating the zoo of a book is different than caging
experience. In the first place, you look out at the world, let a
little of the world back into you, and you vibrate and shiver
and quake until you have to do something, anything, with
this energy. So you make things. Write things. Draw things.
Design things. And all that well before you think about
curating the zoo. The animals of the work come first. The
zoo of the book comes later.

Essay on the personal business of bookmaking in a digital world

Which brings me to business. You may put the art before
the purse, but the purse is also personal. It's your money,
after all. Yes, you made all these nifty animals. Amazing!
Now what? Don't you want to run outside and show your
friends what you made? Yes, indeed. But a shoebox won't
do. So will you pay for the creation of your own zoo? Will
your zoo travel? Can people visit your zoo? Can people buy
copies of your zoo on Amazon? We're talking about money
here. Zoos cost money. Books ain't free. The paper of walls,
the ink of bars, the glue of boundaries.

There are almost too many zoos to choose. Print a zine off
your desktop laser printer. Make copies of your pamphlet
at the copy shop. Make your own chapbook or booklet
or promotional giveaway. Self-publish a paperback with
a vanity press. Use print-on-demand digital presses.
Produce a professional portfolio using a short-run
press. Edward Tufte self-publishes all his design books,
remember, but most of us only have enough capital for a

Keep a safe distance.
Please feed the animals.

cappuccino. You can self-publish at Xlibris, iUniverse, BookSurge, AuthorHouse, CafePress, and Lulu. You can print photo books and art books on demand at iPhoto, Flickr, Snapfish, and others. And you can always hunt for local printing companies who offer quality digital printing for short runs and short funds.

The zeitgeist of samizdat

Because of digital technology and a changing publishing industry, the future of digital-press technology will continue to blur the boundaries between self-publishing, on-demand publishing, and short-run printing. Bookstores now publish their own books. Anyone can publish a single copy of a paperback or photobook using an online service. Soon, digital book presses will be as affordable and portable as color laser printers are now, maybe even more so if Steve Jobs comes out with an iPress someday.

Meanwhile, I have made books a million ways and too often ended up on the wrong seat of the profit/loss seesaw. I always thought I'd at least break even. Don't we all? And when I lost money in a venture, I did what all frustrated entrepreneurs do. I became an artist and called my work a labor of love.

And then I did it again.

So here's a quick survey of love and loss in today's dizzying world of bookmaking. It's fun, but not free. It's artistically liberating and financially ruthless. Success depends on both design wit and business wisdom. And your wisdom can come at the expense of my experience.

o

XLIBRIS. I used this on-demand printer in 2000 to print my first book. This was self-publishing and therefore limited to a kind of self-promotion. I hoped to make back my investment, but that didn't happen. For a fee, Xlibris designs and lays out the book for you, but the company charges way too much for an individual author to recoup his investment. (This isn't the place for entrepreneurial designers, but Xlibris is one of the biggest and an early entrant, so they should be mentioned.) Their books are priced too high compared to other titles. And somehow my Xlibris book kept appearing on Alibris, a used-book online seller, at a fraction of the retail price and even lower

My first book was The Leap & Other Mistakes, *named in honor of the enterprise of publishing the book.*

than the discounted author price. I bought a few of these and confirmed my suspicions that these were new, not used, books: not cool. I now cannot recommend Xlibris to anyone for any reason. I even pulled my book off Xlibris completely, and it's now out of print. (The printing packages at Xlibris.com currently range from $299 to $12,999; no, that's not a typo.)

BOOKSURGE. For my second book, I went with a very small press, and they let me do my own design and typesetting. I set up the whole thing through Booksurge (now owned by Amazon). It was cheaper and still fun, but it was also something I did for the lark of it. I made no money on it. I never used them again, and I can't recommend it. (One funny thing also kept happening, which is perhaps a result of the rather labyrinthine relationships among online businesses: when customers bought the book online at Amazon, I'd receive an email requesting that I pay for the cost of the $9.99 book, a strategy that, the email added, was good for "promotional purposes." What would I have been promoting, exactly? News of my insanity?)

My second book was called The Human Case, *a collection of stories, vignettes, and prose poems.*

One thing I did differently with this book is that I tried to get it into bookstores on consignment. This was possible because a small press published it, and so, while it was print on demand (POD), I could still shelve a few copies with indie bookstores. I sold a hundred or so books. Most were shipped back to me. I never followed up with some of the bookstores. The transaction costs of consignment are simply too great. It costs too much to print the book, make the calls, fill out the forms, ship the books, and then either split the cost 60/40 with the bookstore or pay for the return shipping of the books. In many cases, I just let the bookstore keep the books. It wasn't worth the cost to get them back. I was essentially paying to sell my books, promoting what had become the old news of my insanity.

List of indie bookstores here: newpages.com/ bookstores/default.htm

CHAPBOOKS. For two of my fiction/graphic-art collections, I worked with two small presses to produce chapbooks. Chapbooks are usually one hundred pages or less. They are printed out on a desktop printer, folded in half, and stapled at the spine by hand. Covers may be printed in short runs on a digital press or on cardstock using a desktop printer. These are another hybrid, made possible by stubborn and creative individuals with personal computers, layout software, and spare change, simpatico with the zine ethic. In this manner you control your expenses and earn a little cash by placing your chapbooks with a few select bookstores and, most importantly, by selling them online. As a designer I can heartily recommend this approach because you retain all control, and you are forced to get down and dirty working hands-on and trying to be imaginative with a small to nonexistent budget. Online, you can discover many micropresses, minipresses, and nanopresses so tiny they fit in the palm of your iPod. Start your search at NewPages.com (newpages.com/npguides/bookpubs.htm) and the Independent Publishing Resource Center (www.iprc.org/links.php).

LULU. The new kids on the block of POD are places like Lulu.com. Lulu charges nothing for you to set up your book with them. You need to be very design savvy and have all the software and skill that designing a book requires. But once you design your own book and create your PDFs for the cover and interior, you can order your books one at a time. This per-book cost is still expensive; however, I now use this kind of printing technology for very specific purposes. I print out a few copies of my portfolio. I print photo books that I give as gifts to family or friends. And I print early drafts of my books so that I can proofread the copy and review the cover design and layout. These are great uses of this technology, and they depend on printing very few copies and not trying to earn money off their sale. I don't use Lulu to print books in order to earn money. I can't recommend that. It won't work. But I do recommend using Lulu for these very limited cases. I mentioned Lulu to a design instructor, and he now allows his students to print full-color samples of their work using Lulu's services.

I made a ninety-page photo book of the move my wife and kids and I made from Michigan to North Carolina, and I gave the book to relatives. The advantage a place like Lulu has over online services that offer only templates is that you can design each page with photos, scans, captions, colors, type—whatever you want.

SHORT-RUN DIGITAL PRESS. Many presses now offer short-run work on their digital presses. I have used a few press shops to print my own books, either on my own or with another small press. When I worked for a printing and design company, I never had to worry about the business end of production. Other people worried about that. I just had to complete the creative part of the project. On my own I learned the hard way (which is really the only way) how to negotiate the entire book-printing process, from concept and design to budget and production. As a naive entrepreneur, I had realistic expectations. I spent about $250 to have 50 copies of a paperback printed. That's $5/book—not great, but not bad. And over time I could earn that money back because I controlled the whole production effort, all costs and all income. For a novel, the publisher and I worked with a press shop to take advantage of their digital presses to print an initial short run, and as the first run sells out, we'll print another run, taking advantage of the digital press to better manage cash flow.

This was for Twisted Fun.

This was for American Home Life.

○

I recommend making a print-on-demand book as an expensive learning experience and not as a business proposition. Make chapbooks and zines and anything else using desktop computers (and cheap ink cartridges) and bind the printed works by hand. Use online services like Lulu and others for very limited purposes, like gift books, proofing copies, and limited runs of a portfolio. Sell your books person to person and online through your own websites and via Powell's or Amazon but not on consignment with bookstores. (I still place some books on consignment now and then, but the profit margin is too slim to cover the transaction costs.) And use short-run digital presses when working with a small publisher to get your books into print economically.

See the NewPages *website for lists of indie bookstores, and see the following link for indie comics stores and other bookstores likely to accept your little creatures:* www.indyworld.com/ comics/stores.html.

As long as we keep making our funny little creatures, there will always be zoos. Please visit the gift shop. We appreciate your patronage.

CHIP KIDD

THE TWENTY YEARS OF CHIP KIDD'S CAREER IN BOOK DESIGN HAVE COINCIDED WITH BIG CHANGES IN THE BOOK INDUSTRY. As megachains have out-evolved indie bookstores and as publishers have been absorbed by media conglomerates, the marketing of hardcover books has gone hardcore consumerist, tricking out books into luxury objects and personality accessories. A designer fit for the times, Chip Kidd makes books into coveted objects and conversation pieces, seducing the consumer and flattering the reader.

Review of the book designer's 2005 monograph Book One

Having previously derided the vanity of monographs, Chip Kidd expresses his ambivalence by exposing half of his monograph outside its hard covers. Hold it by the spine, and the pages loll out like a tongue. Playfully suggesting his ego might be overblown, he enlarges a photo of an extra-small book to fit the cover of his XL tome. Having said that a book's contents are more important than its cover, Kidd doubts the value of his book whose contents are *only* covers. Nevertheless, his big book demands a large table and devoted attention, bending readers into the postures of medieval scribes.

Behold the career of Chip Kidd. As faithful to book covers as to his first love, the Knopf art department, since 1986, Kidd reveals in *Book One: Work 1986–2006* that his professional life is as uncomplicated as his designs are unpredictable. Kidd has no regrets about devoting his life to this narrow form and no regrets about staying at Knopf. He duly credits Sonny Mehta, the head of Knopf since 1987, with supporting the remarkable design team still headed

Cover and interior spreads reproduced by permission of the publisher from Chip Kidd, Book One *(New York: Rizzoli Publications, 2005)*

by Vice President and Art Director Carol Devine Carson (Barbara deWilde and Archie Ferguson left the Knopf team in 1999). With a prestigious publisher, encouraging bosses, good budgets, and top authors, Kidd is the farthest thing from an underdog designer at a small press. His struggles have been literary and aesthetic, not economic or bureaucratic. Conceived in freedom, his work inspires, though his fortunate work experience will likely frustrate young designers, inspiring a great deal of career envy. Kidd has, of course, made the most of his luck, enjoying the craftsman's privilege of attending to what is close at hand. One by one, naked manuscripts appear on his desk. Year after year, he covers them.

Book One is a Kidd's meal of book covers with side dishes of shop talk, wisecracks, and authorial blurbs. Strangely, Kidd has been more personally forthcoming in interviews. Rather than revealing himself, defining his relationship to his parents, criticizing his career choices, or doing anything that would be demanded of a writer's memoir rather than a designer's retrospective (he is also a novelist, after all), Kidd reprints photographs and ephemera annotated with jokes ("The problem with Zorro was that it was too easy for my first-grade teacher, Miss Kinsel, to figure out who I was. That bitch."), gushing flattery from authors ("Wherever I go, I'm asked about Chip in reverential tones," writes Donna Tartt, author of *The Secret History* [1992] and *The Little Friend* [2002]), or shallow musings ("Growing up and going to school in Pennsylvania was great, but I'd outgrown it—as for so many others, New York was it for me. Whether or not I was for it was going to be the most daunting problem yet I would attempt to solve."). To be fair, every graphic designer is tempted to substitute the image for the word, the thing for the story. The authors whose books Kidd covers know that writers need to reveal their desire, their pain, their fear. Kidd deflects these questions with his work and his humor.

Kidd's prolific output of cover designs (an estimated eight hundred and counting) proves his passion as much as his talent, and the variety of his output resists general-ization: Kidd is a professional character actor. He reads the scripts of new books, fills his imagination with someone else's personality, and gets as much out of the role as he can on the stage of a book cover. This approach allows him

His first novel was The Cheese Monkeys *(2001). Kidd's follow-up novel is* The Learners *(2008).*

great flexibility. On rare occasions he can outshine the writer, shock the audience, defy the director, and annoy the producer.

Neither publishers nor authors know what sells, and in self-defense, Kidd limits his duty to inspiring browsers to pick up books. Whether they do this is an empirical question that can't be determined by sales figures or author testimonials. The latest book by Michael Crichton, John Updike, Anne Rice, John le Carré, Elmore Leonard, David Sedaris, or Howard Stern is not just another title tossed into the marketplace. Each has marketing muscle behind it: publicity, tours, distribution, dedicated displays at Barnes & Noble and Books-A-Million.

Kidd's unmitigated critical praise in the press is partly due to his success in sustaining an upper-middle-class reader's self-image as intelligent, educated, and hip. His covers charm by paradox, tickle by juxtaposition, and reassure by incorporating photographs, museum art, and familiar things like dolls, toys, and clothing. Kidd's sincere love of pop culture, from *Batman* to *Peanuts*, and his uncanny sense for the bold photographic image or found art equip him perfectly to legitimate the intellectual and economic value of the product.

It makes sense that Knopf has supported Kidd in his efforts to upgrade the hardcover book with die cuts, acetate covers, belly bands, and other packaging technologies, often copied shamelessly by other publishers. It's also easy to see how Kidd occasionally falls victim to the overtly literal, using a pencil for *The Pencil* (1990), ice for *Ice* (2005), the moon for *Lunar Park* (2005), bones for *Rule of the Bone* (1995), and so on. Kidd can also take the found-object collage too far, creating frenetic mishmashes in covers for books by Oliver Sacks, Joan Didion, and John Gregory Dunne. His covers for James Ellroy's novels represent his best work in this much-copied style, combining the close-ups and multipaneling of comic books with true-crime photography.

Kidd will likely remain best known for his earnest upscale invigorations of graphic novels and his talent in pairing photographs with book titles to inspire jarring and mysterious narratives. Our brains are built to leap to conclusions, and Kidd exploits this capacity most brilliantly in his covers for *The Abomination* (2000), *The Little Friend*,

One of these days, someone in a back room at Barnes & Noble will be sitting in front of a bank of surveillance-video monitors and studying the shopping habits of book buyers. Of the women who linger at this shelving unit, how many stare at this particular cover; how many pick up that book; how many study the cover, front or back, for more then ten seconds; how many open the book; how many read any portion of the book; how many buy that book; how many buy another book on that shelving unit; how many are distracted by the noise of children or the smell of a banana muffin?

Magical Thinking (2004), *The New Testament* (1996), and the books of Cormac McCarthy, Elmore Leonard, Dennis Lehane, and David Sedaris as well as select covers for Vertical, a Japanese publisher.

Admired for his best-selling covers, Kidd claims he's most proud of a cover that didn't sell at all. His cover for *The New Testament*, translated by Richard Lattimore, featured a close-up color photo by Andres Serrano of a dead man's bloodied eye, taunting readers with the reality of a historical Jesus. It is perhaps the one cover that maintains Kidd's credibility among designers because it so boldly commits a cardinal marketing sin: never shatter the dream of the consumer.

X FOR ALL OR NOTHING

x BLURS THE LINE BETWEEN LETTER AND THING, BETWEEN SYMBOL AND ACT. So often used as an unknown quantity, a placeholder, it also functions as the signature of an illiterate, a result of slashing at the surface. To X is to mark, and X is the mark. It is the quintessential mark.

X reigns in pop culture as identifier (Generation X, X Games), as shorthand (THX or TX for "thanks" in text messaging), and as the whole word ("X" for the drug ecstacy, or MDMA). But in the abecedarian world of lexicography, the measure of a letter's prestige is the number of dictionary pages devoted to a letter's words. Word count is market share. Dictionary is demographic. Lexy is sexy. And in the dictionary, the X pages are lean indeed.

Essay on the promiscuous Mr. X

The twenty-fourth letter of the modern Latin alphabet is more flexible than its lex-lack suggests. As a noun, X represents the unknown, whether a person, place, or thing. It is also a verb. To X is to mark with an X or to delete, cancel, or blot. (Historically, for, say, signing a land deed, a clerk or lawyer adds the person's first name in front of the X, the surname after, a *his* or *her* above, and the word *mark* below. X is a legitimate signature when a person is ill, blind, incapacitated, or illiterate.) X is also an adjective, familiar to drinkers of XXX liquor (moonshine), wearers of XXXL clothing (*XL* for "extra-large"), and purveyors of X-rated materials (the X rating has been officially replaced by NC-17, although adult films still use the X designation).

As a symbol, X is a strike in bowling and baseball, a defensive player in a football diagram, a kiss at the end of a letter or text message. On maps, X is infantry or mountaintop. X multiplies ($2x2=4$), relates dimension

(2x4), and signifies the unknown algebraic quantity (2x-4x). X prescribes medicine (Rx), reacts chemically (rx), raises a musical note to a double sharp, and refers to pins and lamps in circuit diagrams.

As a creative mark, X checks the box, the ballot, the tic-tac-toe square, and the treasure map. X also closes the Window.

Still, an impatient lexicographer X'd out way too many X words in his sudden hurry to complete his duty. He got to X and cried, "Only Y and Z to go!"

I happened to be flipping from U to Z when the injustice made itself known. X may mark the spot, but its pages are easy to miss. The X pages are lonely stragglers, arriving only after the happening party of W is over, and they are easily overwhelmed and ignored in the rush toward Y. Flimsy and insubstantial, the X pages are an embarrassment to the eye, a disappointment to the fingers.

Yet, we would barely know which way to turn without the x-axis. We simply can't break from X-ray. And none of us would be here without the X chromosome. The other letters may sneer with contemptuous xenophobia at poor little X, but where would those other letters be, typographically, without the x-height? As designers, we are naturally "xeno-philic" (a word not listed in my dictionary's X pages).

So does this deficit cry out for remedy?

If it does, we've more than made up for it in the world beyond the dictionary, the real world of slang and commerce, lingo and branding, movies and nicknames and books and, just, stuff.

In the world of books, X is anonymous and dangerous but also transformative, transcendent. *Mr. X* might take a break from *Project X* to attend *Symphony X* with *Nathalie X* sometime around *Twilight X*. After graduating from *Academy X* on *Earth X*, *Soldier X* might be stationed at *Camp X* and soon deployed to *Planet X* to battle the *Virus X* from *Dimension X*. On *X Day*, *Little X* might play *The Game of X* with the *X President*. If there's *A Warrant for X*, the *X Bar X Boys* are probably *Looking for X*, which will surely end in *The Tragedy of X*.

In the well-panelled rooms of comic books, X functions mainly as the mysterious name of a character (X in Dark Horse Comics, X and Professor X in Marvel Comics) or a team of characters (Marvel's X-Men, X-Force, and X-Statix).

But *X* is also a place (Planet X), a weapon (Weapon X), and the title of a manga series.

In movies and television, *X* suggests secrecy, bravado, and science gone wrong. Mr. X was a character on *The X-Files* as well as in the film *JFK*. Dr. X, or Dr. James Xavier, was a character in the 1963 sci-fi horror flick *X: The Man with the X-Ray Eyes*. In 1998's *American History X*, Edward Norton's character attempts to erase his neo-Nazi past and start over. Ice Cube starts over by playing Triple X in the sequel to *xXx*, in which Vin Diesel played the original Xander Cage. Pre-dating the boys is Agent Triple X, Barbara Bach's character in the 1977 James Bond film *The Spy Who Loved Me*.

As for the spies who worked for a living, MI5 used the XX System (or Double-Cross System) in WWII counter-espionage overseen by the Twenty Committee, which gave the system its name (20 in Roman numerals is XX). Triple X Syndrome is a real chromosomal abnormality in which women have three X chromosomes (one consistent effect is the women are very tall). Syndrome X is a "syndrome" because it puts "60 million Americans at risk for heart attacks," and it's an "X" because it's a "hidden" condition, so says the jacket copy of the eponymous book (2001).

X is a blank placeholder, but it is THE blank placeholder. No other letter quite marks the spot like *X*. A cross. A double slash. A burning brand. It's the way it looks, the innumerable ways it can be replicated, but also the way it sounds in the mouth. *Eks*. Its sound is that of swords crossing, a fillet hitting the frypan, a curse. A hex. It also sounds like a coughing up, like a hair is caught in the back of your throat. *Eks. Eks.* You're trying to get rid of something you don't want. Cough it up. X it out.

Ah, yes, the ex, as in ex-wife, ex-husband, ex-girlfriend, ex-boyfriend. My ex. Your ex. How's your ex? Gone, my friend, long gone. *X'd out*. The shorthand nickname is a way of blotting out the person, the past, the thing. But the saying of it keeps the bitterness alive. The *ex* symbolizes what the nickname seeks to blot out. Saying the past is past somehow keeps the past alive. It's akin to the censor's XXXXX's calling more attention to the words beneath. The *ex* is paradoxical.

Ex also happens to be, in industry, the explosion-proof symbol. Can't live with 'em, can't blow 'em up.

Camp X-Ray was a temporary holding facility for detainees at the U.S. Naval Base in Guantanamo Bay, Cuba. The first detainees arrived January 11, 2002, and were transferred to Camp Delta on April 28 and 29, 2002, at which time Camp X-Ray was closed. Names for the camps on the naval base corresponded to the phonetic alphabet used for military communication (Camp Alpha, Camp Bravo, etc.). On the north side of the base, camp names were designated using the opposite end of the alphabet, hence Camp X-Ray.

And saying it also sounds like the end. The end of something. Something that was but is no longer. A nothing. A nihilistic letter. Comic artists used to use *X*'s over a character's eyes to show death. In Latin, *ex* means "out of," which might be why the word *existence* sounds like its opposite: ex-existence. Ex-ist. I used to be. Now I'm an ex-me. I've gotten over myself, forever.

To name oneself with an *X* or an *ex* is to self-annihilate. It can be destruction for the purpose of creation. A phoenix rises out of the *X*'s. A person reborn as an identity without limitation, without restrictions, without moral code. That's the transformation imagined by creators of comic-book and movie heroes.

In real life Malcom X sought to reclaim his identity by reclaiming his name. Then there's Madame X, the woman who modeled for John Singer Sargent's *Madame X*, a painting that scandalized Paris in 1884; she turned out to be Virginia Avegno Gautreau of Louisiana, a woman who sought to reinvent herself in France. As Roman numeral, *X* identifies you as one in a series, a holder of the ten's place. Pope Gregory X (1271–1276), for example, made his name by writing a letter famously opposing the blood libel: the claim that Jews killed and ate Christian children. ("[W]e order that Jews seized under such a silly pretext be freed from imprisonment.")

And then there's Jesus.

In January 2007, the *New York Sun* reported that Saudi Arabia may ban the letter *X* because "it resembles the mother of all banned religious symbols in the oil kingdom: the cross." The *X* is not a reference to the cross. It does, however, stand for Christ in words like *Xmas*, but only because the first letter in the Greek spelling of Christ is *X:* Χριστος.

I wrote in the marginalia earlier that this was an essay on "the promiscuous Mr. X." I was playing with the idea that *X* as a letter and symbol is used frequently in our language and culture. I have learned there was a real promiscuous Mr. X, made notorious as a subject in the sex research of Dr. Alfred Kinsey. This shows my age. I was born in 1969. Kinsey published *Sexual Behavior in the Human Male* in 1948. I must have heard this before somewhere, probably during a lecture in school, doomed to forget it, but I was recently reminded of it by a chapter, "What I Did at the Kinsey," in

Geoff Nicholson's fun book *Sex Collectors* (2006). Kinsey interviewed Mr. X, or Rex King, a government employee, in 1944. It took seventeen hours to record a sexual history that included heterosexual and homosexual sex with thousands of men and women, sex with animals, sex with seventeen members of his own family, and sex with hundreds of children of all ages, including babies and some of the mothers of these children. It says something about the resilience of the letter *X*, its inherent slipperiness, or perhaps our culture's use of and reliance on *X*, and specifically Mr. X, that *X* can represent an individual like this—a chronic pedophile—and yet not be tainted as a symbol. *X* can escape and live to name again another day.

A year before Kinsey published his book on male sexuality, there was another famous Mr. X. Under the alias "X," George Kennan wrote an article, "The Sources of Soviet Conduct," in the journal Foreign Affairs *in 1947. Kennan detailed the policy that would be referred to as "containment" and would be adopted by the U.S. government with respect to Communist countries.*

X can signify danger and the forbidden. The participants in Stanley Milgram's experiments of the 1960s sat before a series of toggle switches that, when flipped, delivered shocks of various degrees of intensity to people ("learners") who failed to remember matched pairs of words. The learners were actors and were never shocked, but they acted as if they were, grunting, shouting, screaming, and even going silent. The subjects, who believed they were engaged in a memory experiment, were supposed to increase the intensity of the shocks as the learners continued to give wrong answers. The toggle switches had the following labels: Slight Shock, Moderate Shock, Strong Shock, Very Strong Shock, Intense Shock, Extreme Intensity Shock, DANGER: Severe Shock, and, finally, XXXX. This last represented the final level, a lethal shock of 450 volts. Forty psychiatrists polled by Milgram before the experiment guessed that only 1 percent of subjects would deliver the XXXX shock. The experiments, over and over again, showed that 65 percent of subjects flipped the lethal XXXX toggle switch, in many cases after the learners had already gone silent, feigning unconsciousness. Psychologist Philip Zimbardo referred to the XXXX-labeled switch as "the pornography of power." *X* seduces you, even when you should know better.

X can also stand for a group or ethic. The punk-originated Straight Edge Lifestyle is signified by a variety of *X* logos: X, XXX, xXx, sXe, and 24 (X, the twenty-fourth letter). Minor Threat's 1981 song "Straight Edge" condemned drugs and alcohol; sobriety gave singer Ian MacKaye an "edge." An *X* on the back of the hand (see the Teen Idles' cover for their

1981 EP *Minor Disturbance)* derives from a 1980 story that a club owner branded the underage Idles with black *X*'s on their hands.

Coincidentally, and as more proof that *X* can be its own opposite, *X*'s were traditionally used to indicate the strength of an ale. Dos Equis ("Two *X*'s") is a brand of Mexican beer, and XXXX (usually spoken as "Four X") is a brand of beer made by Queensland brewers.

Whether alcohol is involved or not, *X* has often been the easy answer to the hard question of naming bands, songs, and albums. *X* is the name of albums by Klaus Schulze, INXS, The Beloved, K-Ci and JoJo, Queens of the Stone Age, Def Leppard, Anna Vissi, and Liberty X. *X* is also an Australian punk band, not to be confused with The Ex, an anarchist punk band from the Netherlands, or X-Alfonso, a Cuban musician. *XXX* is a 1999 album by ZZ Top, while Triple X Records operates in Los Angeles.

The creation myth of the band Brand X is that a music critic scribbled "Brand X" in the studio diary. That joke on pop culture has given us Brand X Martial Arts, Brand X Internet, Brand X Music Catalog, and Brand (x), a UK ad firm that claims, without irony, to be "(x)ceptional" and to possess "(x)pertise."

In naming, *X* smacks of science and technology. It's cool like a machine is cool, impersonally sequential, simple as a number, and yet its meaning is beyond the ken of the average Joe. *X* is like a password into a secret language, one that may endow the speaker with a false sense of insider expertise by way of a mere facility with the jargon. You don't have to know what it means as long as you say it with confidence.

In aerospace, *X* stands for "experimental," and the culture loves to appropriate the experimental. From NASA's *X-33* Program and the *X-15* aircraft, you get the *X-Wing* fighter from *Star Wars* and the 2006 *X-Plane* postage stamp, which features an image of the *X-15*.

The resonance of *X* as a signifier of mysterious precision explains why it's so common in commerce and branding. The Jaguar X-Type. The 2008 Mitsubishi Evolution X. The X2000, Sweden's high-speed train. The X-Acto knife. Mac OS X. The X game for Nintendo's Game Boy. Microsoft's Xbox console. Vitaminwater XXX (three antioxidants). The

X is a California roller coaster (the seats swivel around).
Product X is a protein powder for bodybuilders. The X-Vest
adds weight for exercise. Very few drug names start with X
(Xanax, Xenical), maybe because that's too scary, but dozens
of others incorporate X into the name (from Aciphex to
Lovenox to Zyprexa).

Check out your local Yellow Pages for companies like
X-treme Car Care, Xpress Motorsports, and Xtreme Tans,
and compare these minimall youth-culture examples
with the high-end Boomer retail incarnation of Paloma
Picasso's X pendant and other X jewelry for Tiffany's. X can
be lowbrow and highbrow, negative and positive. It can
blot and delete; it can select and claim. The sophistication
of X can be appropriated by culture and commerce, but the
simplicity of X can also take us back to our childhoods. X
can be the mark of a child learning to draw. X can recall our
first gestures with a crayon. We remember these gestures
fondly, with nostalgia. In remembering, we perform the
simple miracle of changing X from a *No* to a *Yes*.

汉字 WELCOME

LANGUAGE IS A PUNK. Always messing around, mixing it up, breaking rules. Kids in China are breaking linguistic traditions thousands of years old. They use English words directly, like *iPod, rock and roll, zip it, kick your ass, CD,* and *DVD. KTV* stands for "karaoke," and *MTV* stands for any music video. "To text" is to *SMS. 3Q* means "thank you." New concepts need new words, and young people in China are constantly inventing new phrases and new slang thanks to texting, email, the internet, and video games.

But it isn't just the kids. It's the culture. China has a middle class and a professional class. People travel internationally, work for foreign businesses, shop for trendy fashions. As the culture innovates, so does the language. People in China are changing the way they work, shop, and communicate—and the way they speak.

New technology, especially in communication, drives linguistic innovation. Cell phone is *shou ji* (手机), or "hand machine," and the brand Bluetooth is *lan ya* (蓝牙), or "blue tooth." These are examples of the most common way of creating new words, which is to combine Chinese characters. The word for USB drive is *yo pan* (优盘), a word created partly phonetically (*yo* is close to *U*) and partly by combining a character (*pan* can mean "disk"). HDTV has been adopted as a straight English acronym while *X guang* (X光), meaning "X-ray," is a hybrid word combining a roman letter and a Chinese character. The internet invites all sorts of slang, including *internet friend* (网友) and *kong long* (恐龙) (literally "dinosaur"), the derogatory name for a net friend who turns out to be unattractive.

Essay on new Chinese words, phrases, and characters

"Text message" is 短信, *and "to send a text message" is* 发短信.

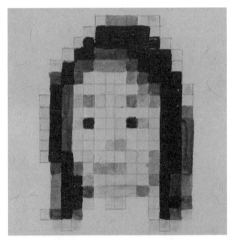

*Mandarin characters
for "net friend," top, and
"cell phone," bottom.
Illustrations
by Louise Ma.*

Some internet slang breaks into popular culture. The neologism *PK* spread from online gaming, where it stood for "player kill," to subcultural slang in which *PK* meant "to challenge" or "to compete" and was used as an alternative to the Chinese expression *tiaozhan*, and finally to the mainstream by way of the popular TV show *Chaoji Nüsheng*, the Chinese equivalent of *American Idol*. Now *PK* is used in magazines, newspapers, and other media.

Another example of mainstream appropriation is the phrase "My turf, I decide," from the song "Wo-de Dipan" (or "My Turf") by the Taiwanese pop star Jay Chou. The song was used in a China Mobile ad campaign targeting young cell phone users, and now it's a popular catchphrase. Its popularity is significant, because it expresses individualism in a culture that encourages conformity.

Businesspeople are using new words (like *ppt* for *PowerPoint*) but only those businesspeople exposed to outside cultural influences. Studying businesses in Beijing, Professor Qing Zhang, of the University of Arizona, found that professionals in foreign businesses drew on international sources to create a more cosmopolitan version of Mandarin while those in state-owned businesses did not. "As a sociolinguist, I'm interested in how language is used to construct new social distinctions in the changing sociopolitical landscape of China," says Professor Zhang, who also observed, in her 2005 article "A Chinese Yuppie in Beijing" *(Language in Society,* 34:3, 431–66), that the use of a cosmopolitan Mandarin did not just reflect social differences but created them.

Zhang uses the term cosmopolitan to convey the idea that the professional's language was no longer provincial but international. Use of a cosmopolitan language expresses a yearning to belong to a new "higher" class.

Which brings us to shopping, where language has always been used to create in-groups and out-groups, inspiring consumers to be hip to the latest cutting-edge trend. A measure of China's move to a consumer economy may be found in the weekly TV show *S Qiangbao Zhan* (S Information Station), with the *S* referring to *shopping*. The show caters to young professionals and promotes the latest furniture, accessories, fashion, electronics, beauty products, and sports gear. Its slogan is *"jiang* shopping *jinxing daodi,"* meaning "carry shopping through to the end." It's a play on the communist Mao slogan, "Carry the revolution through to the end." Yes, Maoist revolution has been replaced by shopping.

Zhang wrote about her analysis of the TV show in a 2006 article entitled, "Jiang Shopping Jinxing Daodi!: Linguistic Innovation and Social Distinction in Chinese Television Medium."

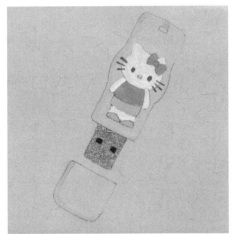

Mandarin characters for "USB drive," top, and "green," or "sustainable," bottom. Illustrations by Louise Ma.

Professor Zhang studied sixteen episodes of the show, tracking the language used by the show's two hosts, Liu Ling and YuYuan, who used new words and expressions from mainland Mandarin, Taiwan Mandarin, Hong Kong Cantonese, English, and even Japanese. "The innovative linguistic style used by the hosts to project hip and cosmopolitan personae," says Zhang, "is composed of new Chinese expressions, English expressions, sound features and grammatical features," all of which the government prohibits.

The government requires that the language used in broadcast media be Mandarin, based on Beijing Mandarin called *Putonghua* (Mandarin is the official language of mainland China, which excludes Hong Kong and Taiwan; Beijing is the capital city, and Beijing Mandarin is the official government-sanctioned Mandarin). The two hosts of *S Qiangbao Zhan* are not supposed to mix foreign languages or imitate other accents, dialects, or styles of expression; but they do. They use English, abbreviations, hybrid words, and various tones and dialects. They use contemporary international vocabulary, like *hongxi hu* for "coffee brewer," *jingyou* for "essential oil," *kü* for "cool," *xiangxun liaofa* for "aromatherapy," *kiu* for "cute," *meimei* for "pretty girl" (originally online slang), *wa* for "wow," as well as many English words directly, like *download, email, DIY*, and *hip-hop*. These words have Putonghua equivalents, but the hosts use English to show they know what's hip.

It's always tough to know what's hip in any country, but it's especially tough to keep up with the lingo in China, where the basic linguistic principles are pretty complicated. Westerners are often confounded by the use of Chinese characters. The blog Hanzi Smatter (hanzismatter.com), founded by Tian Tang in 2004, is "dedicated to the misuse of Chinese characters in Western culture," which often means tattoos that don't mean what you think they mean (one that supposedly meant "courage" really meant "serious mistake"). The Western temptation to extract literal meanings from Chinese characters is misguided.

"Chinese characters are a means for writing Mandarin and are not themselves a language, no more than the Roman alphabet is itself the English or French or German language," cautions Mark Swofford, who lives in Banqiao,

As any hipster knows, even nerds can mimic slang, but it doesn't make them hip. In advertising and marketing, language styles are often used to create the perception of in-groups and out-groups and to inspire the out-group to try to belong by imitating in-group language first and habits of consumption second. This is pretty much the dynamic going on in China now as a whole, as it has in so many other consumer cultures. Kids, consumers, and professionals are using language to create in-groups defined as new, contemporary, international, high-tech, and high-class, in order to distance themselves from the old, traditional, provincial, rural, low-tech, and low-class.

*Q: A friend said
newspapers printed in
Chinese characters can
be read by people who
speak Mandarin or
Cantonese. How can
this be?*

*A: When people are
taught to read and
write in "Chinese,"
they're taught to read
and write in Mandarin.
But speakers of
languages other than
Mandarin use different
pronunciations and
make other adjustments
(syntax, grammar,
phrasing) to understand.
Written Cantonese is
different than written
Mandarin, as is written
Taiwanese, but most
people don't know how
to read those, as they're
never taught. Consider
how someone literate in
Italian but not Spanish
could nonetheless make
out a great deal of a
Spanish newspaper.
Think of how the word
lingerie is pronounced
in English and French,
though written the same.
Various pronunciations
for Chinese characters
means that Chinese
characters aren't a good
fit for the languages, and,
of course, it makes them
a real pain to learn.
—Mark Swofford*

Taiwan, and runs the website Pinyin.info, which explores the Romanization of Mandarin. "You're likely to come across something like this: 'The Chinese word for *computer* is made of two characters, one for *electricity* and one for *brain*. So a computer is an electronic brain.' This is wrong. Chinese characters are not building blocks that can just be assembled."

Mandarin words are disyllabic and require more than one character to write. Mandarin has 405 syllables, and each may be read in four tones. Of these 405 syllables, 297 have a single meaning while the rest have at least two separate meanings, often corresponding to several characters. Many characters do derive from pictograms (for, say, *human*, 人; *the sun*, 太阳; *mountain*, 山; and *water*, 水), but by far the majority of the tens of thousands of characters represent phonetic syllables. Most speakers get by knowing two to five thousand characters. Many characters are semantically related, often with identical syllables, and that's why the same word can be written several ways with different characters. In Mandarin, as in all languages, meaning depends on context: on words, phrases, sentences, and inflection, as well as on the circumstance in which the language is written or spoken.

New words can be created phonetically, like *fen si* (粉丝) for *fans* (as in sports fans) and *sha fa* (沙发) for *sofa*, but dialects complicate matters. Thomas Talhelm, a high school English teacher in Guangzhou (he picks up the latest slang from his students), remembers a Korean student who was surprised that Thomas didn't know what a particular three-character word (麦当劳) meant since he was, after all, American. In Mandarin, the word *Mao Dang Lao* made little sense, but in Cantonese phonetics, it sounded more like *McDonald's*. "Similarly," says Talhelm, "a popular chain store from Hong Kong, Watson's (屈臣氏), sounds similar in Cantonese but nothing like it in Mandarin, in which it's *Qu Chen Shi*."

Beyond dialect differences, it's often difficult to express a new concept, like *green* for "environmentalism," which can be translated literally as "green" (绿色), as in "a green Olympics" (绿色奥运会). Lisa Weir, who moved to Shanghai in 2006 after graduating from the University of Michigan with a degree in English and who now works for New York University in its study-abroad program, says *eco-friendly* can be expressed as *hao de huan jing* (好的环境), which means "good environment." But she relies on the aphorism *"Bao hu huan jing"* (保护环境), meaning "protect the environment."

"This is what I tell the ladies at the local store when they look at me funny after I've refused the plastic bag for my bottle of tea," says Weir.

When a new concept has become so integral to modern life, maybe it's time to do what is almost never done in the Chinese language. Maybe it's time to make a totally new character.

"Take, for example, the radical for *water*," says artist Jiao Yingqi. "There are 470 words using this radical. This reflects the importance of agriculture in the past. Now we're in the information age, and computers are increasingly important. The Chinese expression for the *computer* alone requires two characters. Without a radical for the *computer*, it's difficult to condense other words related to the computer or the internet."

Jiao has created several new characters (*xin hanzi*). The one for *pollution* is a combination of the existing radicals for *air* and *poison*, which he pronounced as "wu," the same sound as the word for *dirty*. The *wu* radical could be combined with other characters to create words for vehicles that pollute, people who pollute, victims of pollution, noise pollution, light pollution, etc. Jiao's radical for *computer* is a square in the middle to represent the monitor, a long cross stroke under the square for the keyboard, and a dot on the right for the mouse. For his *money* radical, Jiao uses the symbol for the Chinese currency, *renminbi* (¥), to form new words expressing "slush fund" and "people who are obsessed with money," as well as money-related crimes, economic predictions, and other concepts. Going even farther, Jiao has called for "personal *hanzi*."

"Creating words is the responsibility of all Chinese users," says Jiao. "That's the case with users of English, French, and German. As a society China doesn't much acknowledge the value of the individual. It's up to the country to overcome this barrier."

Character? Radical? Pictogram? Pictograms or ideograms refer to those characters that pictorially represent an idea or whose origins lie in pictorial representation (e.g., the character for tree might express the original intent to graphically depict a trunk and branches). Ninety percent of Chinese characters don't work like this. They're more like morphemes, representing a syllable, like "yi," and don't really mean anything. And the word radical is tricky. Sometimes a radical is a meaningless slash or stroke within a character, and sometimes it's the whole character with a meaning (e.g., an ideogram). Sometimes it can be a morpheme, a syllabic unit.

The character for "new," or xin, is 新. The characters for "characters," or hanzi, are 汉字. And the characters for "new characters," or xin hanzi, are 新汉字.

HERE COMES THE ROOSTER

THE ROOSTER AIN'T GONNA DIE. The Year of the Rooster drew to a close, but the rooster, as a symbol, doesn't really need its own promotional campaign. Through the centuries, it has remained a persistent poult.

During the 2005 Year of the Rooster, the rooster appeared on coins, stamps, and casino chips. It also appeared on the usual suspects: t-shirts, stationery, and calendars.

Special year or not, the rooster lends its likeness to bands (Little Red Rooster), restaurants (Red Rooster), songs ("Rooster Blues," Lonnie Johnson; "Little Red Rooster," The Doors; "Rooster," Alice in Chains), movies (*Rooster Cogburn* [1975], starring John Wayne and Katharine Hepburn), motorcycles, tea kettles, mailboxes, coffee mugs, cookie cutters, paper-towel dispensers, Pez dispensers, chewing tobacco, quilts, Halloween costumes, Provence fabrics, specialty plates, lamps, logos, welcome mats, giant commercial statues, and just about anything else you can imagine.

The rooster can be suggested with a few simple strokes: a body with comb and tailfeathers will suffice. A mere doodle begets its cock-a-doodle, by which we mark our morning rise. Or else the rooster evokes nostalgia for the pastoral ideal. Or pride shading into vanity. Boldness. Home cooking. Virility. We associate its image with just about anything but the beast itself.

o

*Exterior anatomy of the
rooster. Illustration
by Kimberly Battista.*

Some facts about the beast itself:

1. Roosters are bred for show, kept as pets, and still trained illegally for cockfighting.

2. Young roosters are called cockerels, and castrated roosters are capons. A cock is a male bird, not necessarily a chicken. There are dozens of poultry breeds: Araucana, Brahma, Cochin, Delaware, Frizzle, Houdan, Jersey Giant, Minorca, New Hampsire Red, Orpington, Plymouth Rock, Rhode Island Red, Silkie, Sultan, and Wyandotte—just to name a few.

3. Roosters may be slaughtered for consumption, but what we usually consume, as meat or egg, is the white Leghorn hen. We also eat Plymouth Rock hens and Cornish cocks. They are the most efficient meat-producers. We also eat Jersey Giants and a variety of broiler breeds (birds bred to produce meat for consumption) whose DNA may come with a patent. The majority of our white eggs comes from the Leghorn hen, or at least the hormone-boosted factory-farm superhen that lays 250 eggs a year. Other egg layers are the Rhode Island Red and the New Hampshire. Meat chickens are also boosted with hormones and whatnot to grow chunkier faster, and, as opposed to grain-fed organic poultry, factory-farmed chickens eat what we eat: other chickens.

Many consumers are becoming squeamish about factory farms, disease, antibiotics, pesticides, herbicides, hormones, etc., and are increasingly buying the organic, the free range, the randomly drug-tested (if a star layer is hitting over three hundred, it's time to pee in an egg cup).

4. The rooster, while it produces sperm from a testicle, does not possess a penis. It has, instead, a cloacal opening, like the hen.

5. In 2007, according to the USDA, over nine billion chickens were slaughtered in the United States.

From the "Poultry Slaughter Annual Summary" published in February 2008 by the National Agricultural Statistics Service of the United States Department of Agriculture (USDA)

o

IF YOU CONSIDER INCORPORATING A ROOSTER INTO A DESIGN, YOU MIGHT WANT TO DIG INTO THE FACTS, HISTORY, AND LEGENDS OF THE ROOSTER. You can slap together a generic symbol, like the lame-o logos for the Red Rooster and Chick-Fil-A restaurants, but

*Digestive system of the
rooster. Illustration
by Kimberly Battista.*

a generic rooster doesn't exist. The variety of breeds may provide inspiration, tweak a tired icon. For beautiful photos of poultry breeds, check out the 2003 book *Extraordinary Chickens* by Stephen Green-Armytage. For background broad and deep, check out *The Chicken Book* by Page Smith and Charles Daniel, published in 2000. A wealth of birdy information can be found in Ernest Ingersoll's 1923 *Birds in Legend, Fable and Folklore*. It is out of print, but the entire text may be found online at www.archive.org.

As for references in religion, literature, law, and astrology, let's get to it.

For entertaining facts about the poultry industry, read Eric Schlosser's 2001 book Fast Food Nation *(e.g., McD's and KFC are the country's largest buyers of chicken; 90 percent of the chicken Americans eat has been chopped up, as in nuggets; eight chicken processors control two-thirds of the market).*

o

A LITTLE LIGHTNING

For many ancient peoples—the Iranians, the Aztecs, the Chinese, the Japanese, a few tribes in Africa—Earth in the beginning was like a yolk in the egg of the universe. According to the Luyia people of Kenya, god made a great red rooster who lives in the clouds and sends lightning when it shakes its wings and thunder when it crows. In southern Africa, lightning is a bird that lays an egg where it strikes, and people who are struck by lightning are said to have been scratched by the claws of the bird. One of the Penan tribes of Borneo took a cock with them wherever they went in the forest so they could pluck his feathers and make offerings to the thunder god, Baléi Liwen. Mog Ruith is a Druid who wears a speckled bird-costume and can conjure storms at will. The association of roosters with lightning and storms brings us to *The Waste Land* by T. S. Eliot:

Only a cock stood on the rooftree
Co co rico co co rico
In a flash of lightning. Then a damp gust
Bringing rain.

A LITTLE PROPHECY

Roosters swallow small stones to help them digest their food. In ancient Rome, people believed a cock could have a magic gizzard stone, which they called "alectorius." It supposedly granted men strength, courage, money, women, and the power to become invisible. "Alectromancy" was the

Q: Uh, why in the world
do you know all this
stuff about chickens
and roosters?

A: I wrote my first novel
from the point of view of
a rooster. I did a lot of
research, little of which
ended up explicitly in the
novel. The research did
inform the novel
in other ways.

name for a certain brand of augury in which practitioners relied on roosters to help them predict the future. Cocks were considered "birds of the sun," and Babylonian priests would put their cocks on the altars before they made their offerings. Even today farmers try to predict the weather from the scratching of chickens. In the 1970s, researchers in New York stuck a chicken in a wind tunnel because tornadoes in the Midwest sheered off chicken feathers, and these geniuses figured they could index the force of tornadoes by counting feathers.

A LITTLE ASTROLOGY

Those born in the Year of the Rooster possess the following qualities: honesty, ambition, curiosity, confidence, good judgment, self-reliance, courage, fear of commitment, and dedication. Roosters are also eccentric deep thinkers and moody loners who always think they're right. The Rooster's color is white, signifying purity and maturity, and the Rooster's ideal partner is the Ox or Snake.

A LITTLE LEGEND AND RELIGION

The Medes were an
ancient Iranian people
who established their
own empire in the sixth
century BC. The Vendida
is said to be their
religious text. Refer to
Ernest Ingersoll's Birds
in Legend, Fable and
Folklore (1923).

In the *Vendida* of the ancient Medes, the cock calls men to their religious duties. If the cock crows before dawn, according to Hebrew legend, it is to warn the faithless. A statue of a cock atop a church tower alludes to St. Peter as the head of the Church and embodies the voice of the Church, calling on men day and night to repent.

In Greek myth Athene blinds Tieresias because he sees her naked, and his mother Chariclo begs Athene to give him back his sight. Instead, Athene endows him with an understanding of the language of birds. God taught David and Solomon the language of birds. The spiritual meaning of the story of the cock and hens in the Gnostic texts—the texts were found in the early 1900s on expeditions led by Albert von Le Coq to the Taklamakan desert of Central Asia—has not been preserved or is no longer discernible.

I referred to The Kama
Sutra of Vatsayana
translated by Sir
Richard Burton and
F. F. Arbuthnot,
published in 1995 by
Wordsworth Classics.

Of the "64 practices that form a part of the Kama Shastra," which, with the Kama Sutra, were written to instruct women, number 41 is "Arts of cockfighting, quail fighting and ram fighting." Chapter IV, "The Life of the Citizen," prescribes that after breakfast the householder should teach birds to speak.

A LITTLE LITERATURE

Reynard the Fox, a mischievous hero of medieval epics, flattered the proud cock to lure him to dinner. In the 1390s Geoffrey Chaucer wrote of the heroic rooster Chauntecleer in "The Nun's Priest's Tale," included in *The Canterbury Tales*. In "The Fighting Cocks and the Eagle," Aesop described a victorious cock being nabbed by a swooping eagle and concluded that "pride goes before destruction."

More approving of the virtues of the rooster, François Rabelais, in his masterpiece of the 1500s *Gargantua & Pantagruel*, explained that Euclion's cock "by his scraping discover'd a Treasure" and that the crowing of a cock was said "to astonish and stupify with fear that strong and resolute Animal, a Lion."

In *Hamlet*, Heraldo claims it was the crowing of a cock that awoke "the god of day" and scared away the "erring spirit" of Hamlet's father just as the ghost was about to speak.

In *Walden* (1854) Thoreau writes: "I do not propose to write an ode to dejections, but to brag as lustily as chanticleer in the morning, standing on his roost, if only to wake my neighbors up."

Writing in a chapter in *The Descent of Man* (1871), Charles Darwin observes: "It may perhaps be objected that the comb and wattles are ornamental, and cannot be of service to the birds in this way; but even to our eyes, the beauty of the glossy black Spanish cock is much enhanced by his white face and crimson comb." Later Darwin writes of the rooster that "beauty is even sometimes more important than success in battle."

Chickens have been crossing the planet's roads for 150 million years, and now their poultry parade continues in the virtual ether at poultry.org, on Wikipedia, and anywhere else the sky is fowling.

With a slogan like this, the rooster is the new mascot for graphic designers.

A LITTLE LATIN

Gallinaceous means "of common domestic fowl." In Latin, *gallus* means "cock"; *gallina*, "hen"; and *gallinaceus*, "of poultry."

A LITTLE FRENCH

The emblem of the old fighting Gauls was the cock. In the 1200s, there was an order of knights who called themselves *L'Ordre du Coq*. After the French Revolution, in the late 1700s, the First Republic installed the cock on its flag. In 1804, Napoleon replaced it with a Roman eagle. When Napoleon left for Elba, Louis XVIII resurrected the Bourbon lilies, and after Napoleon's return and defeat at Waterloo,

Louis Philippe reestablished the iconic primacy of the old Gallic cock.

A LITTLE LEGAL HISTORY

In Switzerland a man's cock could corroborate his courtroom oath of self-defense in the killing of an intruder. Silence was deemed corroboration. If the cock spoke, it would be interpreted as an objection, and the man's story would be disbelieved.

See Walter Woodburn Hyde, "The Prosecution and Punishment of Animals and Lifeless Things in the Middle Ages and Modern Times," University of Pennsylvania Law Review 64:709 (1916).

A LITTLE GENDER BENDING

In 1474, a rooster in Basel, Switzerland, was tried, convicted, and burned at the stake for the heretical and satanic crime of laying an egg, a feat we know today to be biologically possible.

It has been documented that Romanian farmers fed their roosters alcohol-soaked grains to induce them to sit on eggs and brood. Drunk roosters become motherly.

For a perspective on categories from the chef's point of view, see gourmetsleuth.com/ chickens.htm. For the vegetarian's perspective, see www.vegsoc.org/ info/broiler.html. And from the perspective of the chicken accused of a crime, know your rooster rights by checking out www.animallaw.info/ articles/dduschick.htm.

A LITTLE MEANINGLESS CELEBRITY

Celebrities born in the Year of the Rooster include: Michelle Pfeiffer, Britney Spears, Catherine Zeta-Jones, Goldie Hawn, Deborah Harry, Yoko Ono, Steve Martin, Spike Lee, Eric Clapton, Neil Young, Johann Strauss, and William Faulkner.

A LITTLE ANECDOTE ABOUT HARRY TRUMAN

In the Truman Home in Independence, Missouri, the seat cushions are still on the chairs at the kitchen table where President and Mrs. Harry Truman ate breakfast together. After he was done being president, he came home for good and continued to have breakfast and even lunch there, at the table, with Mrs. Truman. On each of those well-worn seat cushions is an image, in profile, about the size of an opened hand, of a red rooster.

A LITTLE CONCLUSION

The rooster has had a long strange journey as a symbol. Designers may be tempted to be reductionist when using its image, perhaps because so few of us live within earshot of the cock's morning alarm. And yet the rooster will still be heard, one way or another.

RED & YELLOW KILLS A FELLOW

I'LL HAVE A DANGER BURGER AND HAZARD FRIES.
To glow, please.

Why do we use red and yellow to alert us to fast food
and danger? Red/yellow says, "The food's good here and
pretty cheap too"; and, out of the other side of its signifying
mouth, cries, "Watch out! Trouble ahead!"

Essay on why red and yellow signify both food and danger

The National Fire Protection Association uses color-
coded warnings in which red indicates flammability
and yellow indicates reactivity. The U.S. Department of
Transportation identifies the Pantone colors for its traffic
signs, reserving red (187), yellow (116), and orange (152)
for the most important cautionary signs. At the same time,
hundreds of fast-food joints and cheap eateries rely on the
red/yellow/orange combo, their exit-ramp signs blooming
from Seattle to Shanghai. If you jumble these signs together,
the Toxic Hazards with the Taco Palaces, you'd be unable to
distinguish one species from another based on plumage.
You'd need words and context.

So do we instinctively associate danger with these colors?
After all, Mother Nature warns us with the red and yellow
of the poisonous coral snake: "red on yellow kills a fellow;
red on black, venom lack," goes the old saying. If not by
instinct, then perhaps by experience we learn to associate
danger with red and yellow. Either way, do fast-food folks
bait us with danger colors and then switch to assuring us of
the proximity of rice noodles and cheesesteak?

One 1989 theory posits the reverse: mammals developed
the ability to distinguish between red, yellow, and orange in
order to identify ripe fruit. Fossil evidence suggests early
primates lived on a diet of fruit, and a 2002 study showed

human vision to be better adapted to perceiving fruit scenes
(pictures of apple trees and berry bushes, for example) than
other random nature scenes. If this is true, then do we
glimpse the red of a stop sign and salivate for cherry pie?
And why, then, are poisonous snakes and frogs as brightly
colored as any still life by Matisse? Fortunately, the brain
doesn't encode experience with the binary inflexibility of a
machine. We are more than what is dreamt of by primates
and professors.

We read signs in context. So maybe red and yellow are
popular for just plain standing out against the background.
Traffic signs pop against the brown and green of the highway, and burger beacons shine against the cloudy skies
above exit ramps. In eye-level clusters, however, they're a
mess, mixing with the other colors of the surburban sprawl
and urban glut, industrial gray and minimall brown. And
besides, highway signs are also blue, green, and brown;
commercial districts feature signage of more hues than seen
on the Cartoon Network; and regardless of background, red
and yellow show up helter-skelter on other kinds of logos,
from the Marines to the red-hawk logo for my high school
and from DHL to Shell Oil.

Every culture imbues its colors with positive and negative connotations. Yellow is joy and cowardice, the color of
oak-tree ribbons and jaundice, Asian spirituality and Egyp-
tian mourning. Red is love and vengeance, valentines and
spilled blood. In China and India, red symbolizes good luck
and celebration, while in other countries, red stands for
socialism and slasher films. Everywhere, red and yellow are
the fireworks of autumn. Red and yellow can be as beautiful
as the robe of a Chinese emperor and as ugly as the dollops
of ketchup and mustard on a cold beef patty.

Still, there's no denying the overwhelming consistency of
red/yellow/orange in the realms of danger and food service,
which is interesting given that the color with the least
universally negative connotations is blue. Maybe there's
something to the slightly ugly look of red and yellow. It's
candy corn and hot sauce but not fine dining, jewelry stores,
or anything upscale. If red and yellow stand out, you watch
out. If they stand out and look cheap, then it's time to eat.
Pick Up Stix, for example, is a franchise Asian restaurant
whose reds and golds, according to its executive director of
marketing, "reflect spice, flavor, and heat."

Fire. A-ha. *Fire burn hand.* Bad. *Fire cook meat.* Good. Even
cavemen understood the duality of fire and, thus, the life and
death symbolized by flames of red and yellow. It's possible
restaurants resort to the colors of cooking flames while
danger signs scare us with simulated infernos. The majority
of logos don't depict literal flames, perhaps because fire by
itself doesn't necessarily mean food. Fire could represent
hell or arson or a custom car paint shop. And it's doubtful
most customers think of flames when confronted with
blocks of red or washes of yellow. It's the glaze of grease,
not the blaze of brush fires, that red-and-yellow restaurant
logos bring to mind.

○

But this, too, begs the question. Do we glimpse, out of the
corners of our eyes, that snatch of red, that blur of yellow
and reflexively look to determine fire or food, hazard or
hamburger?

"Colors are constructs of the brain, not physical
realities, and the presumption would thus be that whatever
color or color combination is most appealing to humans
is attractive because of some ecological/evolutionary
advantage," explains Dale Purves, M.D., director of the
Center for Cognitive Neuroscience at Duke University.

"While the current evolutionary arguments are interesting, they suffer from being purely correlational," continues
R. Beau Lotto, PhD, of University College London. Colleagues Lotto and Purves (with Surajit Nundy) coauthored
the general-audience neuroscience book *Why We See What
We Do: An Empirical Theory of Vision* (2003). "We've no
idea whether the pressure that drove the evolution of our
receptors was the ability to detect ripe red fruit on green
backgrounds, since there are so many other potential cor-
relations one could find. There's even a study suggesting
we adapted to detect blushing. The receptors of bees are
maximally tuned to detect the 'colors' of flowers. However,
rather than the eye adapt to flowers, current evidence suggests it was just the reverse: flowers adapted to be detectable
by bees and other insects/birds. It is nonetheless true that
we can detect some wavelengths better than others, simply
because of the physics and physiology of our extant system.
Why this is so isn't known."

Purves and Lotto argue that how we see depends as much on experience as on eyeballs. To avoid being tricked by optical illusions, we judge what we see now against what we've seen in the past. That is, we interpret visual cues against our experience. Scientists might not yet know why certain colors are such strong visual cues for us, but they do know that we can learn to attach meaning to certain color combinations.

o

We see color in order to recognize things faster and see them better. So argues Karl R. Gegenfurtner (Department of Psychology, Gießen University in Germany) and Daniel C. Kiper (Institute of Neuroinformatics, University of Zürich in Switzerland) in their article "Color Vision" (*Annual Review of Neuroscience* 26 [2003]: 181-206), which surveys past visual experiments.

Our ability to detect color helps us see objects, distinguish elements in our environment, and improve our memory of what we've seen. We see color early in our visual process, at the stages of the retina and lateral geniculate nucleus (LGN), where the color signals (in three separate color-opponent channels) are transmitted to the cortex.

Gegenfurtner and Kiper argue that *many* areas of the brain, rather than a single devoted area, work to help us perceive and process color information. "Concerning early processing," says Professor Gegenfurtner, "it is known that people have vastly different ratios of L- and M-cones (red and green cones), but they all have pretty much the same unique yellow. It seems like the system is self-calibrating."

And what about red?

A. Chaparro, C. F. Stromeyer, III, E. P. Huang, R. E. Kronauer, & R. T. Eskew, Jr., "Colour Is What the Eye Sees Best," Nature 361 (1993): 348–50.

"I don't really know why red is such a good warning signal," he says. "It might have to do with the extremely high sensitivity of the red-green system. In fact, Charles Stromeyer and his colleagues from Harvard have shown that the eye is best suited to detect small red (or green) spots of light."

o

While scientists continue to explore why we notice certain colors more than others, the explanation for the Jekyll/ Hyde symbolism of red and yellow might lie more in our culture than in our craniums. So can we blame McDonald's for linking red and yellow to fast food?

Before McDonald's, red and yellow had a cautionary history in the United States. Highway departments required in 1924 that caution signs have black letters on yellow and in 1955 that stop signs have white letters on red (durable red paint wasn't available until 1954). The first lone McDonald's opened in 1940 in San Bernadino, California, and catered to drive-up customers. In 1948, it ditched the carhops and delivered the world's first fast-food burgers. In that same year, Nels Garden, one of the heads of the University of California Radiation Laboratory in Berkeley, objected to yellow as a background color for the newly designed radiation symbol because yellow was too commonly used as a warning. Testers cut out the three-bladed radiation symbol (evoking sun rays) in magenta and stuck them to colored cards twenty feet away. A committee chose magenta on yellow as the best combination. In 1953 the first pair of golden arches was built as an architectural flourish into the second McDonald's restaurant in Phoenix, Arizona. Ray Kroc launched the franchise in 1955. In the early 1960s, the arches were incorporated into the logo.

McDonald's grew into a global behemoth, begetting thousands of red-and-yellow fast-food children all over the world. When confronted today with blank blobs of red and yellow, most people might think "Big Mac" before they think "traffic warning," "radiation," or "fire hazard."

With McDonald's having spread the red-and-yellow gospel, maybe other fast-food joints decided to ride the golden coattails. And once fast-food joints asserted their red-and-yellow identity, turning red and yellow into the colors of fast food and cheap dining in general, restaurant newcomers might recognize the value to be gained by sticking with the pack. Red and yellow logos alert drivers and passersby to fast-food rows all over the world, from Denver to New Delhi.

"For those companies that don't have strong brand recognition, the me-too approach is hard to go against," acknowledges Leslie Harrington, principal of LH Color, a consulting-and-research firm that helps companies better use color in their products and brands. "It would be very hard for the smaller restaurants on Main Street, USA, to challenge the paradigm. It's also difficult for McDonald's to ever change, because they created the monster. They're in the same boat as UPS, which owns brown whether they like it or not."

The uniformity of the global McDonald's brand has likely colored the brand of global fast food. The widespread use of red and yellow may reveal as much about the peculiarities of our culture and the neuroscience of our vision as it does about the economics of our habits.

If there's one lesson to be learned, it's this—if fast food endangers our health, we can't say the colors didn't warn us.

LEFT WANTING

MAGAZINE DESIGN CAN EMBODY LIBERAL PRINCIPLES. I don't know *how* design might express cultural tolerance, underdog sympathies, and the expansion of individual rights. I do have the impression that not a single liberal magazine is giving it a go. Why are liberal magazines so conservative?

Essay on why liberal magazines embody such conservative design

Three reasons: (1) lack of money; (2) the desire for stability; and (3) design-phobia.

1. LACK OF MONEY

Liberal magazines don't have money, and they don't want to appear to have money. "No political magazine in America has ever made money, because advertisers don't want to be in contentious magazines," says Milton Glaser, who worked on redesigns of the *Nation*. "It's important for these magazines to look frugal."

Frugality in appearance presumably evokes ascetic intellectualism. Many political magazines are thin and printed on cheap paper, and obey a structure familiar to anyone who has marched through the *Marine Corps Gazette:* two-column layouts of dense type and one or two inset photographs. Serious photojournalism is rarely featured, and illustrations are restrained, if they exist at all. A Danish newspaper will take the heat for printing satirical cartoons, but an American political journal won't. American editors must believe that while stories look like frogs on the page, when kissed by the reader, they become princes in the mind. But a reader has to work up the nerve to kiss a frog.

The humble look of liberal magazines from the *American Prospect* to the *Washington Monthly* may have its roots in a nostalgic nod to the soapbox orator. "I am defensive of those little political magazines," says James R. Petersen, the former editor of *Playboy*'s "Forum," an eight-page op-ed insert modeled on political magazines. "Words were important. They conveyed the message and kept the crucial facts in front of you longer than the evening news. For me, the pages of *Reason* and the *Nation* were like your local park. You knew the 'soapboxes' and the orators likely to be on top of them, and so you kept coming back."

A lack of money doesn't excuse lazy design anymore than it would excuse lazy journalism. "Money doesn't always give you results," argues Mirko Ilic, who has illustrated covers of the *Village Voice* and, with Glaser, wrote the book *Design for Dissent* (2005). "A designer with ideas, passion, and very little money can do it." And there is a cost for insisting on posing in a shabby suit. "Many liberal magazines take transformative aspirations and render them lifeless," says Brian Awehali, editor of the low-budget, radical-left *Lip Magazine*.

2. DESIRE FOR STABILITY

Liberal magazines want to express ideological commitment through design stability. "It's in the nature of ideological magazines to suggest constancy," says Glaser. "Magazines have specific historical references, and they serve their readership. The *Nation* is polemic, less elegant, with lower production values, and it has a sense of being noisy and aggressive. My struggles with redesigning the *Nation* through the years have always been with the prospect that any proposal for change will be deeply resisted. Trends change, but they want to tell you that their ideologies don't."

A conservative design of a conservative magazine achieves a coherent result. But freezing liberal ideas within a stagnant structure contradicts the message. "There are no liberal magazines," says Ilic. "Left-leaning media bend over backwards to please the center. I was born in Bosnia, and I know you can never please any extreme group, left or right, until you are 100 percent with them."

3. DESIGN-PHOBIA

Design-phobia afflicts even the best editorial minds. "The staff often has strong journalistic skills, but the art of magazine making—clarifying information, supporting stories visually—is not particularly valued," says designer Jandos Rothstein, assistant professor of graphic design at George Mason University.

Ilic is blunt. "Change is hard, and in the meantime they are all crying out for change of government, of country, but they are not starting with themselves. People from inside the magazine are so bogged down fighting bureaucratic crap, they have no outside perspective. If liberal magazines cannot be revolutionary, then who?"

"The magazines are all about changing the world," confirms art director Rhonda Rubinstein, with a light tone. "But changing the magazine is a little too much for editors."

Editors of these magazines tend to come from other liberal organizations—academic, literary, and journalistic. With their backgrounds, they often distrust contemporary visual media, if not graphic design itself.

"We have to be careful, those of us coming from the design community, because we have different values," warns Glaser. "I disagree that all magazines are susceptible to one illness. Products are reflective of single editor with an attitude."

One attitude shared among editors of liberal political magazines (possibly political magazines in general) is that they tend to regard the real estate of the blank page as too valuable to surrender to what they consider "gratuitous" imagery. But what's gratuitous about photos of Abu Ghraib or the first Iraq war's so-called Highway of Death?

"*Life* magazine had the most profound political effect on my life," says Petersen. "The evolution of man, the antiwar movement, the burning monk, the girl running in Vietnam, the police chief executing the Saigon prisoner: those photos are what move your conscience. That's what's missing from all these liberal magazines. I wanted to run, in the pages of *Playboy*, images from the Highway of Death during the first Iraq war, showing what America did to those people, but I was overruled. No one I know ran those pictures."

"The last great liberal provocative artwork I saw was by Micah Ian Wright, who redid the WWI and WWII propaganda posters as contemporary satire," says James Petersen. "I was not allowed to run them in the pages of Playboy. The very courage that made Playboy the first national magazine to oppose the Vietnam War is gone in today's climate." Wright's 2004 book If You're Not a Terrorist...Then Stop Asking Questions! (*Seven Stories Press*) includes a foreword by Steven Heller.

"Editors are nervous about the introduction of visual ideas. They are afraid that visuals misrepresent facts," explains Glaser.

"A picture of Abu Ghraib is worth more than ten thousand words," says Ilic.

Reintroducing photojournalism was part of Rubinstein's redesign of *Mother Jones* in 1999. "Up until then, *Mother Jones* was couched in nice, polite design. I wanted to make it more visible and relevant, appealing to the next generation's visual literacy."

o

As for today's generation of upstart magazines, many of them deny the liberal label.

"I take 'liberal' as an insult," says Awehali. "*Lip* is not in that category."

Awehali is in good (and venerable) company, as even Art Director Stacey D. Clarkson says, "We at *Harper's* magazine don't consider ourselves a 'liberal magazine' but, rather, a vehicle for critical thought and fine writing." And Jason Kucsma, founding copublisher of *Clamor,* concurs: "I don't consider *Clamor* to be a liberal magazine. I consider it to be a radical leftist magazine that appeals to a wide range of left-leaning individuals, from academic liberals to direct action activists."

Today's activist magazines are less concerned with the great American liberal experiment than with expressing an anticorporate critique and satisfying a civic-minded, not necessarily political, youth culture. But they take design seriously.

"I grew up reading the *Nation,* the *Progressive,* and *Z Magazine,* and I was disappointed," says Kucsma. "I was disappointed by their utter lack of attention to creating something that is even remotely visually engaging. I wanted to work on a magazine that was politically radical *and* aesthetically engaging."

Magazines don't have to change if they don't want to. The design of liberal magazines can be properly conservative, in certain cases. But that doesn't make it natural law for all magazines. A liberal magazine can espouse liberal principles in its design and grow, over time, into a stronger personality engaged with the world. If you take both design and liberalism seriously, surely this presents an opportunity?

"I absolutely think that it's possible for *Clamor's* personality to be embodied in the magazine,"says Kucsma. "One of the key components to *Clamor's* identity is that it is a lot of things to a lot of different people, and we try to reflect that in the way the magazine is put together. We question ourselves about how representative our images are of the community of people reading the magazine (or the communities we would like to have reading the magazine). I'm talking about gender, ethnic, and economic representation primarily. Do we publish pictures of mostly white guys while our articles are usually written by more than 50 percent women? Do we focus on photos of stereotypically attractive women when we have entire sections devoted to challenging dominant gender roles? Those are the sorts of questions we're asking. And we work with artists to do illustrations with a wide range of cultural experiences and work/illustration experience."

Clamor *has gone defunct, while* Good Magazine *has entered the fickle fray of the marketplace.*

o

Timid political art. Stale design. The money excuse. The market dynamic in which political speech is toned down for a presumably thin-skinned public. Artistic cowardice masquerading as commercial sensibility. These are the charges, but what is the role of design in political magazines? Is it to perpetuate a stylistic template? To signify stability?

There are always excuses for the status quo, and while excuses might rationalize, they don't really justify. Some magazines *do* have money. *George* attempted the celebrity/lifestyle treatment for political life, for example, and *Good Magazine* is doing for citizenship what *Seed* has done for science. So money can only be part of the equation.

If editors took design seriously (and deferred to the designer's expertise in fitting form to content), then why shouldn't the magazine's design embody liberalism's principles: change, progress, growth? Why the staid, sober, stagnant look of conservative newsweeklies when they might choose to express something far more vibrant and forward-looking? If you looked just at the magazines, you might feel the fight was lost long ago.

"Design is order, economy, teaching people beauty, creating individuals," says Ilic. "Good design is subversive. And because it's subversive, good design is left wing."

Liberal magazines can be seen as members of a commercial species, finches that have adapted to fit their niches in the Galapagos of the newsstand marketplace. Or they can be seen as members of an editorial species, dodos that have adapted themselves into a corner, flightless and awkward. Commercial adaptation is a kind of tautological cop-out, a brand of self-serving determinism ("the market makes us do it this way"). Editorial adaptation is fueled by choice in a circumstance of uncertainty. There is the potential for bravery here, for self-determination. Commercial species adapt out of fear, to survive indefinitely. Editorial species can adapt out of hope, to thrive—and to risk dying out.

A magazine that embodies evolutionary principles? A scaly tabloid evolves into a feathered website.

What design often does is to put form in service of content, and if the content is liberal, shouldn't the design (over the lifespan of the magazine) express in some measure liberal ideals or principles? If not, then a static, restrained form suggests by its appearance that political magazines are in essence conservative: that is, resistant to change. If the magazine merely preaches to its choir, then its mission is not so much a liberal one but rather a tribal one. The magazines look and operate more like community newsletters rather than like liberal magazines for a national audience. The whole idea of a liberal magazine in this context becomes wonderfully full of paradox, especially if you consider the many who *do* share the ideals of these magazines. A sober, newsy, dense, and retro design turns these readers off—not because they're young but because they're far more tech savvy and design literate and ad aware. We know our Edward Tufte as much as our *Wired* magazine, and we're well aware that everyone is selling us something.

Yes, "wonderfully" full of paradox. I like and root for these magazines, and who doesn't trust paradox and contradiction more than stubborn orthodoxy?

Readers deserve to be challenged, not tasked with déjà vu. Of course, some people only trust the familiar. Perhaps a conservative resistance to change is an expression of the American style of governance—the balance of powers keeping political change behind the curve of culture. The job of the liberal magazine may be to mark a symbolic place, mimicking a community without asking its readers to incur the cost of participating in one.

But liberal design could yet invigorate a liberal magazine. Directed evolution, rather than stagnation or revolution, could shape the magazine's identity over time. Like a personality or a government, a liberal magazine could work for political change while grudgingly admitting to change in itself. Maybe I've composed a mission statement for a magazine that doesn't yet exist. In the meantime, liberal political magazines champion conservatism by design.

NEW U?

RIGHTEOUS WHINERS. Desperate losers. Defensive liberals. Those who call for social justice are often made to sound like shrill complainers. Consider unions. Say *union*, and a young person today imagines a white middle-aged pot-bellied factory worker, a stereotype representing a blue-collar middle class diminishing in size and strength every year. The future of unions depends on the service industry, essentially on the likes of the young people who regard unions as dead. Unions have a serious graphic image problem.

Essay on the design of graphics for labor unions

Unions seek social justice for the worker, and social justice depends on compassion for those left out. The movements for the civil rights of women and minorities rallied supporters by asserting the value of compassion. Today's social causes promote compassion, but they recruit members by getting people to admit they need help. To seek strength in your union, you have to admit weakness in yourself. People don't like doing this. Maybe people don't admit to being in the working class because they hope to escape it.

How do unions present themselves today?

COLOR

Blue rules. The colors of the American flag are as omnipresent in union literature as they are in political-campaign literature, but a quick survey of the printed materials and websites of several unions (AFL-CIO, United Auto Workers [UAW], Teamsters, National Writers Union, Graphic Artists Guild) reveals that blue is the color of choice. Are unions consciously using blue to represent the democratic "blue states"? It's possible, but it's more likely that the blue mood predates the red/blue divide. Sticking with a red, white, and blue motif, unions reject too much red (evocative of Communism) and up the blue (more conservative, literally).

TYPE

Sans serif, brothers and sisters, all the way. Futura is no-nonsense, modernist, industrial. Helvetica is a workhorse. Universal ain't no Ivy League sissy. Unions take pride in their gritty urban origins. Nostalgia for their hard-knock tradition is sustained in simple, clean, thick, stand-up type. Some periodicals distributed internally to members can be downloaded in PDF format from union websites (see the website addresses at the end of the essay).

DESIGN

Union design, thy name is Grid. Concerned not with looking good but with working straight, union design relies on grids, columns, boxes of blue, and blocks of quotes, anything to fill up the space. Union magazines are like newsletters. Their straightforward look promises solid information, not corporate candy and public-relations puff pieces. Anything artsy is suspect. If it looks too good, it's either lying, selling something, or trying to make people feel stupid.

PHOTOGRAPHY

Respect the worker. The purpose of union photography is to feature people, not products. Union photography promotes solidarity among all workers by depicting portraits of diversity: black, white, Hispanic, old, young, male, female, etc. Diverse people cut out and arranged against backdrops of patriotic colors attempt to sustain America's vision of itself as a melting pot of all peoples. A sample cover from the March–April 2006 issue of the UAW magazine *Solidarity* features one white male, one black male, one white female and one black female.

*Cover of the March–
April 2006 issue of
the UAW magazine
Solidarity, distributed
to members of the
United Auto Workers*

o

Unions have so much going for them. They have hard-working people, real stories, a cause. They're underdogs. Their leaders are democratically elected representatives accountable to their constituents. They have American authenticity in a way that corporate marketing departments could never concoct.

So why does the union's look feel outdated, untouched by popular culture? Its stodgy and desperately sincere look may reinforce the distance young people see between life on an assembly line at a Chrysler factory and life on aisle three of a Costco supermarket. Compare unions with companies, and unions appear to lack a sophisticated up-to-date visual language capable of rising to the rhetorical challenge. Many union leaders admit their message fails to register with younger generations, but they also admit they don't know why. The Service Employees International Union (SEIU) uses purple and gold to achieve a more youthful, approachable look, but it relies on the same tropes of photography and design as the industrial unions. Unions date themselves by walking and talking like grumpy grandparents. Young people think: "Yes, but what does this have to do with me?"

I've done writing and design for unions for ten years, and while I've had a good view from the sidelines, I don't have a grand remedy. The fiercely adversarial relationship between unions and businesses has long since been replaced by a joining of interests (profit sharing, for one, and job security tied to keeping the company competitive). In the old days, hard-hitting cartoons and caricatures were as common as actual hard hitting. Today many unions are in a bind, and it shows in their restraint (graphically and thematically).

Unions could decide to do what companies do, that is, take more design cues from popular magazines, movies, and television programs in an attempt to reach the younger Wal-Mart/Target/Starbucks demographic. As for content the examples of the satirical newspaper the *Onion*, the satirical cable programs *The Daily Show with Jon Stewart* and *The Colbert Report*, and even viral videos provide lessons on how to connect with your audience by making fun of the enemies of common sense and the Constitution. Jon Stewart presumes you share his point of view and leaps to expose the witlessness of those in power. Stephen Colbert satirizes neoconservative attitudes by pushing them to extremes. They do what Democrats and unionists and Michael Moore have not been able to do: make Republicans and corporate

apologists look like old pot-bellied humorless has-beens—
that is, like parents.

If you want people to join your team, you can make it
uncool to be on the other team. You can turn economic
weakness into cultural strength. You can turn compassion
into outrage, and outrage into laughter. The question
remains whether unions can turn individual laughter into
collective action. Do they need a hip new magazine called,
simply, *U*? Ads on TV, radio, and billboards that make
joining a union seem as cool as playing in a punk band and
as adventurous as joining the Marines? New logos, jackets,
slogans—in short, a complete overhaul? They could make
the other team look uncool, but they still have to make their
team the one to join.

*Many union magazines are available in PDF
format on their respective websites.*

ACLU: www.aclu.org
AFL-CIO: www.aflcio.org
Graphic Artists Guild: gag.org
National Writers Union: www.nwu.org
SEIU: www.seiu.org
Teamsters: www.teamster.org
United Auto Workers: www.uaw.org
UAW-Chrysler: www.uaw-chrysler.com
UAW-Ford: www.uawford.org
UAW-GM: www.uaw-gm.org

EXPLANATION: CRUTCH OR CATALYST?

SHOULD A DESIGNER INCORPORATE AN EXPLANATION
WITHIN THE DESIGN ITSELF?

I've done it four times, all four times on covers for books
of fiction; and I wish I'd done it on two more. Once, I wrote
a fake quote on the back cover. I intended it as a placeholder
for a quote to come, but I didn't want to drop in nonsense.
So I wrote a myth about the illustration I'd done, in effect
explaining the design to the client. They liked it so much
they kept it, and in my heart of hearts I craved this all along.
Another time, I snuck in a poetic introduction on the credits page that set out the themes embodied on the cover. I did
this because the client needed me to explain my cover, and
so I thought his readers might appreciate an interpretive
boost as well. Again, the client liked it and kept it. The other
examples are more of the same. Sometimes the explanation
is on the cover itself, literally within the design, and sometimes it resides nearby in a note or introduction.

Essay on explanations within designs as well as outside designs. Essay includes digressions possibly more entertaining than the thesis, the conclusion of which is pretty much: it depends.

Is this humbly helpful or artistically arrogant?

I think it's artistically helpful, but whether it's humble is
debatable. Probably not. I think I do this out of a complex
of motivations, expressed variably as, "I'm afraid no one
will get it" or "My idea about my design beats the heck out
of my expression" or "Why not?" In my case I was up front
with the clients and let them make the call. I never scrawled
a secret message on the hull of the client's ship. If a client
appreciates it, maybe their audience will too.

A book reader expects to break a sweat in the gym of
interpretation. Yet rarely are explanations worked into
book covers. Browse the shelves and try to find one. No
go. Mostly you get the reproduction of an artwork ("Ooh,
nice blobs" or "Is this a reference to Vermeer?") or else a

pretty darn literal expression of some aspect of the contents
(sepia rowboat floating on placid lake = moody memoir
about fear of intimacy; ornate border around cropped
portrait of woman in sari = if you like Jhumpa Lahiri, please
make this the next selection for your book club). Outside
of the textual playfulness of offerings by the likes of Chris
Ware or McSweeney's, books just don't take chances with
complicating a message.

o

I look at books, think about books, browse bookstores.
And, wow, book covers are sensational, yes? A book cover
today is like a miniature version of a designer's bed on
Sunday morning, revealing in its exquisitely wrinkled satin
sheets exactly how responsive and gentle and thorough a
lover this designer can be (albeit working alone). Other
than recognizing how hot the cover is and, by extension,
how much enthusiasm was lavished upon the work beneath
these rumpled sheets, most readers are not prepared to
spend time interpreting cover designs. Most covers look
elaborate enough so that a book buyer is not embarrassed to
be seen carrying the books to the counter (there are cringing
exceptions). But beyond that, the reader expects the writing
itself to carry the weight of meaning. Book covers are, to the
participants on the bed, the lingerie balled up on the floor.

o

As a writer, reader, and designer, I am tempted to drop words
into my designs. Perhaps this is why: because as a reader I
am more comfortable receiving my complex messages in
words rather than as symbols. It is what I'm used to. It is
what I want. And so the more words that help me interpret
a set of symbols, the happier I am. Incorporating an
explanation into the design of a book cover may operate as a
simple means of reaching an audience. Design explanations
might be dimly uncontroversial in this admittedly narrow
case. Let's go beyond books for a moment.

o

To clarify, let me set out what I'm not talking about. I'm not talking about client presentations in which the designer defends the value of the design. "I made this blue because you guys are so conservative." No. And I'm not talking about the design equivalent of running a shooting range, arming the members of the committee with the interpretive Glocks by which they can blow away each of the thirteen logos except one—that one, there, a little tattered but still clipped to the wire. In fact, Scott T. Boylston, a professor of graphic design at the Savannah College of Art and Design, nicely expresses the dynamic of design defense.

"Presentations have a powerful potential to influence the client's appreciation of the work. That's why they're clients: they need others to help them grasp their own vision. In my experience, some designers, when they present their work, seem to lose their audience. So I've pushed my students to build strong cases for their work *before* showing it, and it is amazing to see how much faster the visuals click for the audience. Sometimes a visual construct immediately prejudices a person, and to set them thinking before they see the work helps direct them toward what they're *actually* seeing, not what they think they're seeing."

How to defend one's design in the client's courtroom is the subject of another essay (by someone else). I'm also not talking about design monographs. A pragmatically inspiring monograph (meaning, it made me want to go make stuff right away) like Martin Venezky's *It Is Beautiful...Then Gone* (2005) depends for its existence on the premise that designers enjoy explanations of designs. Essays, interviews, personal reflections, confessions about the joys of experiment and process—it's all there. And the writing functions, more or less, as explanation. Designs are cool, but they're not enough. That unresolved tension between design and explanation is one of the most interesting paradoxes embodied by design monographs and design writing in general. (How many times have you seen a magazine undergo a complete redesign and *not* explain itself?) For a discipline in which so much stock is put into clear communication, design sure inspires its share of those who believe that clear communication still needs deciphering.

Thank goodness.

o

Design need not communicate clearly. By embodying tension and contrast and ambivalence, a design may excite one's desire to explore the mystery and forge a definition. If a design sparks this desire, you might want to actually own it and develop a relationship to it, perhaps an emotional one or else one in which the emotion gets all used up and the thing gets tossed in the trash. Who can predict?

Design that needs deciphering isn't *necessarily* good design, but the best design demands it.

By which statement I now fear I have let the bear cub of Great Design out of its cage to bound up on the sofa with me. So be it. What is good design? Good design meets your client's needs and satisfies your client enough to pay you. Good design is about today. Great design? Great design is something else. Great design may be unrecognizable initially as design. It may look useless or weird or extravagant or odd. It may look like something else. The great design of tomorrow may appeal to more senses than merely sight: it may smell or move or touch you or talk back. It may change the way we interpret time or space or beauty. It may demand that we make new neural connections in the brain. I know that sounds scientifically reductive, but it is true. Great design is something we don't understand when we first confront it. Great design might make us want to understand it, but it doesn't have to. It will wait for us to come around and find new ways to appreciate it.

To those who presume that if you have to explain a design, the design has failed, is this response: phooey. One goal for the designer is to create something that inspires many competing interpretations so that your design will live a little longer, if only in the obscure writing of lonely critics.

○

I'm also not talking about designs *as* explanations. Please see Edward Tufte for that. Visual explanations, as Tufte argues, masquerade as fact, confound us with misinformation, falsely reassure us with the appearance of an inevitable narrative. (How can you argue with a graph?) Designers may avail themselves of the misuse of visual explanations by incorporating them, satirizing them, debunking them. Very quickly we plunge into the various -ologies of interpreting signs and statistics—the frenetic conversations of our culture. A designer may incorporate these kinds of explanations into the design or offer them up as keys to the design (a translation key on a Sagmeister CD, for example, enables you to decode the liner notes but doesn't reveal a means to interpret the design, which isn't necessary, which is my point). In most cases I can think of, the design-as-explanation isn't intended as a guide to the interpretation of a complex visual message. They are more like map keys or assembly diagrams or secret codes, all intended playfully or seriously, but in the end their use is clear. Literal. Uncomplicated.

o

Here's some of my thinking about explanations *within* the design. (I really should come up with an epithet for this. Organic explanations? Word droppings? Forget it.) Okay, so I think the controversy for me lies more in the gratuitous use of explanations or, perhaps, the uses that more explicitly relate to artistic interpretation, that is, the relationships between symbols. Let's bring up art. Art since at least the time of Duchamp has depended on explanations external to the artwork for its meaning. Without explanations a viewer struggles to appreciate the art and locate the work in some kind of context, some kind of historical relationship. Without gallery guides, critical essays, or art-history classes, I would have little means to grasp the significance of the last sixty or so years of art. Without this foundation, in other words, I see only pretty colors or ugly dogs, washes of light or scraps of paper—same as I see when walking down any street. Big deal.

So my point. Explanations are not new, not crazy, not unheard of. I feel I have to say this to preempt the designer's instinctive objection that design is not art and that any design that needs an explanation has failed. My own sense is that explanations, in some figurative, poetic way, can free the designer to realize some more complicated, sophisticated, ambivalent, and probably more artistic means of expression. It might be that *explanation* is a misleading term suggesting some dry block of 7-point type in the lower right corner. I mean something rather more elegant and sophisticated than that. Perhaps poetry, myth, allegory, a quote, a joke, a subtitle, a panel series in a comic format, maybe something worked in like collage, or a reference to another work, something that might even expand the meaning of the work rather than explain it. It should be nothing like a mission statement or academic thesis. It should be more like a candle of suggestion than a hammer of finality.

I guess I'm also suggesting that meaning can be severed from the object (book, movie, event, product) and nested in the design (cover, website, poster, packaging). The book covers on which I incorporated explanations did not depend on the content of the books for meaning. I may have started with a relevant theme of love or games or travel, but this was only a starting point. After that, I tried to bolster the designs as semi-stand-alone carriers of meaning. Whether or not I have failed at this does not detract from the value of the intent: losing a race doesn't make racing bad. The explanation process might have practical benefits too. If my explanation for a design is dim-witted, then maybe my design is dim-witted. If so, I can dispose of the design and start again. I can design with a more interesting, vibrant explanation in mind. My design can embody a more complicated and satisfying story. This process of explaining serves as self-editing, but its utility can be transformed into a cousin of art by its expression within the design. Read the book, don't read the book. The design still means something. (If only to me, but isn't that always doomed to be the case?)

This is perhaps what is most controversial: incorporating explanations into a design not to reach an audience, not to embody another's message, but instead to assert an independence of meaning for the design itself.

And is this at its core a spiteful means by which I assert my independence? Am I declaring mutiny on the bounty of the client/designer relationship? Am I even describing design anymore? Or am I getting riled up for nothing, this whole thing being rather less inflammatory than my ego would like, it being just another of the thousands of options that one may use or not use according to market demand? (And is that marketing kind of talk forever tautological and thus incapable of ever saying anything at all about anything?)

So, should a designer incorporate an explanation within the design itself? Is this humbly helpful or artistically arrogant?

Explain yourself.

Or don't.

EDWARD TUFTE

EDWARD TUFTE IS DESIGN'S CHAMPION OF REASON. His principles of scientific rationalism are old school, but his expressions of analytic design are sophisticated, smart, and painfully relevant. Eight years in the making, *Beautiful Evidence,* Tufte's fourth book, makes a soberly brilliant case for renewing responsibility in design.

Review of the designer's 2006 book Beautiful Evidence

Professor Emeritus at Yale University, Tufte has taught courses in statistical evidence, analytical design, and political economy. Over the years he has examined a wide variety of visual explanations—from Galileo's notebooks to charts in *Nature* magazine—and posted his findings on his website, spurring discussion among his many faithful readers. His prose can be dry, awkward, and jargon filled ("What are the content-reasoning tasks that this display is supposed to help with" might be rewritten, for example, as, "How can this display help us think?"). His prose can be forgiven, however, because *Beautiful Evidence* showcases Tufte's wide-ranging eclecticism while grounding itself with a genuine and serious respect for truth.

Adhering to principles of observation over superstition and evidence over sensationalism, Tufte is a friend of science and statistics, a rational idealist who presumes that truth is a shared social value. When a newspaper prints a photograph of Saturn, Tufte would add an image of Earth for size comparison. Where a nightly newscast would display a spiking line graph in shocking red, Tufte would add values and a reference to a mean over time. Where bar graphs abound and pie charts predominate, Tufte would wipe the messy slate clean and bring proportion and clarity to our media-driven infoglut.

*Cover and interior
spreads reproduced
by permission of the
publisher from Edward
Tufte,* Beautiful
Evidence *(Cheshire,
CT: Graphics Press LLC,
2006)*

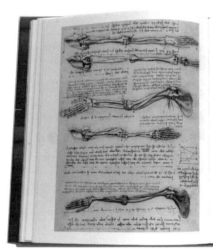

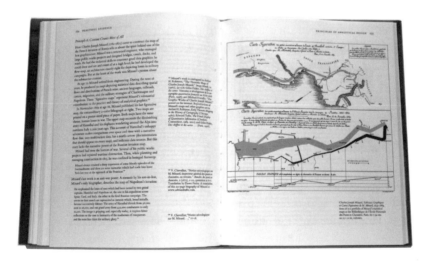

Divided into seven main chapters (the last twenty-four pages are devoted to sculpture, including Tufte's own), the book proceeds with a case-study method. Tufte examines specific designs for their virtues and vices and extracts general rules. He appreciates the elegant integration of text and image as much in a field guide to birds and a report for detecting concealed weapons as in Leonardo da Vinci's notebooks and Galileo's *The Starry Messenger* (1610). In the chapter "The Fundamental Principles of Analytical Design," Tufte derives his rules for good design from rules for good thinking. He identifies expressions of these rules in Charles Joseph Minard's data map of casualties during the French invasion of Russia in 1812.

Tufte's first principle is to show comparisons, and he then explains how Minard's map "makes several vivid comparisons," most notably the difference between the size of the army at the start of the campaign (422,000) and the size, six months later, at its finish (10,000). Tufte uses the remarkable map to illustrate his other principles, including to show causality, to show multiple variables, to integrate words and images, and to provide documentation of sources and authority.

These common-sense rules are controversial for being so widely ignored in print and broadcast media, in online news sources, in medical journals, textbooks, and legal documents. In every chapter Tufte takes pains to point out instances of design negligence, from NASA's PowerPoint presentations on the 2003 Columbia disaster to a graph, originally published in *The Dragons of Eden* (1977) by Carl Sagan, showing the relationship between brain mass and body mass for twenty-six animals.

Tufte walks his talk by improving existing designs. In the second chapter Tufte examines "sparklines," meaning "small, high-resolution graphics," or "datawords." His first example is a patient's glucose-level number. By itself, the glucose level has little meaning. Tufte adds context—a data line of the past eighty readings—and a gray band on top of the data line to show the range of normal readings. In this way a patient can quickly see their current level compared with the history of their past levels relative to the normal limits. Tufte then seeks to improve the design—and thus the meaning—of sparklines for currency-exchange rates, mutual-fund performance, and baseball win/loss records. The designs of sparklines vary depending on context and content, but the principles carry forward into other applications.

Tufte's improvements are sensible. His sparklines pack a lot of information into a small, clean package. His redesigned charts clarify and contextualize. He even describes the tools and capabilities of the perfect PowerPoint killer. Why aren't more information designers doing what Tufte is doing? We defer too often to the slick tropes of pseudoscience, aided by Microsoft's PowerPoint (Chapter 7 in Tufte's book) and abetted by the nightly news. As an academic and an independent thinker (as well as a self-publisher), Tufte contributes a needed corrective to reckless information design. We depend on evidence to persuade us of an understanding, and we use this understanding to guide our judgments about belief and behavior. We need to bring a rigor and a respect to the graphic depiction of evidence of all kinds.

DANGER MUSE

DESIGN IS THE INTENT OF THE MAKER. Today virtually everything expresses a designer's intent: the genetic make-up of your filet mignon, the vanilla-scented atmosphere of the restaurant, your pharmacologically enhanced libido.

With so much design pushing itself into the public eye, the critic must look—and push back. Hazards abound: *ad hominem* attacks, self-aggrandizement, the temptation of a handy but unfair pun as a deadline looms ("Eyeland Castaway: Designer Overbored?"). Some hazards, though, uniquely plague design critics.

Essay on avoiding common hazards in the practice of design criticism

LISTS

The media love to rank the ten best blops, the number-one frip, the hundred greatest pippadoos. In the August 2005 *Esquire*, the subtitle for the product survey "The *Esquire* Ten" reads: "There is power in things. The right things." The value judgments inherent in these shopping lists are not criticisms. Instead, a critic interprets a work and explains to the public why it, in particular, and design, in general, matters. The critic selects but doesn't rank. The public may want a buyer's guide to fraggadorps, but the critic is obliged to compose a thinker's guide to design. In this sense all critics are contrarians.

Magazines allow consumables to roam throughout their pages, but they cordon off design criticism into departments, if they include it at all. Design criticism should not be confused with product showcases or with design journalism.

SHOPPING

Consumers who buy tobacco-flavored toothpaste have every right to fill out nasty feedback forms, but that doesn't make them critics. Consumers need only to open the magazine, turn on the TV, walk through the store, and speak their minds about what they know best: their own consumption. Critics are consumers too, but the greatest hazard of being a critic is to equate it with being a consumer. The consumer experience counts, yes, but critics don't think with their credit cards. And they're not personal shoppers.

To buy or not to buy? This is the consumer's dilemma. For the critic to adopt the binary attitude of a consumer is market madness, a forfeiture of purpose. The critic respects the design as a work within a context, created by an authority, disseminated to the public. The critic asks not, "Is this for me?" but, instead, "Why was this made?"

IDENTITY CRISIS

Design critics tend to be self-appointed. Who am I working for? Who appointed me? Myself, on both counts. The trouble starts when I doubt my value as a critic. (Doubt is one of the default mindsets of the critic; another is envy.) How does this happen? It might happen when a critic confuses criticism with consumption. If design can be consumed, and everyone's a consumer, then we can all be design critics.

This self-defeating logic deflates the critic's ego. In his essay "What's My Motivation?" (*Emigre* 64 [2003]: 101–2), Shawn Wolfe defines his identity crisis as an ambivalence between the personal and the professional: "Actually I felt ashamed for thinking [that redesigning a gum wrapper] mattered at all in the first place.... It's silly, but I'm a designer and can't help but notice these things." His ambivalence arises from a conflation of the consumer perspective (it's just a gum wrapper) with the designer perspective (I care about design), and it's an ambivalence all too easily shared by design critics. In the January/ February 2005 issue of *Print*, Grant Widmer cites as a virtue of a photo book that it never lets "savvier-than-thou design criticism interfere with their world of fun." A design critic bad-mouthing design criticism? Now there's evidence of an identity crisis.

Full of self-doubt, the critic sabotages her own opinions with the plastique of qualifiers and the tiger trap of self-deprecation. In the May 2005 issue of *I.D.*, book reviewer Nancy Levinson admits, after citing the defects of a Phaidon title: "I do hate to be a spoilsport." In the May/June 2005 *Print*, book reviewer Colin Berry quips, after citing the defects of *Graffiti World* (2004): "But who cares?" And the indefatigable Rick Poynor, reviewing *The Push Pin Graphic*

(2004) for *Eye* 54, confesses: "It feels churlish to complain about such an enjoyable book."

These reflexive apologies reveal a charming paradox: the design critic doubts the legitimacy of criticism but stands in awe of its power to affect sales. The critic yearns to strike with confidence and hit the target and yet doesn't want to hurt anybody. Where does this lack of critical confidence come from? I put the question to Nancy Levinson, the director of the Phoenix Urban Research Laboratory, College of Design, at Arizona State University.

"The apologetic impulse springs from a version of the old saying 'Those who can, do; those who can't, teach...or criticize,'" suggests Levinson. "Creating something in the world—a building, a book—is complicated, while criticizing it is comparatively easy. But there might be something else at work. Classic works of criticism—like those by William Hazlitt [1778–1830] to George Bernard Shaw [1856–1950] to twentieth-century figures like Lewis Mumford [1895–1990] and Clement Greenberg [1909–1994]—are products of their time. To be a critic back then was to be an authority, and they trafficked in gnomic certainties, in big-picture pronouncements. So maybe the apologetic tic of modern critics follows partly from our more pluralistic leanings."

If critics want to acknowledge a plurality of value systems, they shouldn't ask, "Who cares?" They should answer, "I care, and this is why."

VENTRILOQUISM

The design critic does not let the businessperson, academic, journalist, or even designer speak through her. The design critic resists the lingo of the scrutinized subject and favors the language of criticism. The design critic does not overidentify with her subject. The critic must remain an intermediary between the design and its audience. A critic can't do this properly if she adopts corporate-speak, design-speak, academic jargon, or the third-person neutrality of journalistic recounting.

Critical language is nimble, flexible, ambivalent, theoretical, personal, rambling, and occasionally contradictory. Design a brochure or corporate identity, a first-aid kit or a stun gun, and you aren't, as a rule, encouraged to contradict yourself, mix messages—be for smoking as well as against it, be for your company as well as suspicious of it, hide the stun gun beneath the antibacterial bandages in the first-aid kit. (As a consumable, a design may express a designer's intent while still being subject to misuse by the consumer who, say, uses a screwdriver to puncture her neighbor's tires.) As a general rule, however, designers make one choice and communicate one message.

A critic is not a designer. Therefore, a critic is not obliged to paddle in a pond circumscribed by a client's guidelines. A critic can make three interpretive choices, explore tentative propositions, and purposefully muddy the waters. Critical writing is not catalog copy, a mission statement, or a technical white paper. Criticism adapts language to its revelatory purpose.

MINDLESS AUTHORITY

Design has a problem with authority. The measure of a designer's creative authority varies widely among projects. Clients exert final control and take full credit. Designers often prefer anonymity, especially when the design sucks. Ignoring sticky questions of relative authority means crafting slick fictions and upholding the pretense of a designer's creative control. Calibrating relationships among members of a design team and client representatives presents a troubling matter of empirical inquiry—the findings sure to be as lively as a judicial ruling on a multiparty negligence suit. Rarely will we have the patience for that degree of parsing.

Critics, however, can't resort to simple appreciation of the object. Critics need an authority in whom to invest intent. The art critic has the artist; the literary critic, the author. With design, the intent is complicated by diffused authority. Its creation is likely to be collaborative, not just between client and designer but between committees of clients and teams of designers. Critics confront the thing itself and often a dizzying roster of contributors. To avoid this difficulty, critics employ the passive voice, imparting to the object its own intent to be whatever it is: "The design is intended to be used," etc.

Another hazard of being a design critic is the temptation to write an essay on the hazards of being a design critic.

Intent, however, is the main character in the critic's story and, like any main character worth following, invites scrutiny as it defies summary.

Good criticism is like good fiction: it makes you wish the characters were real.

MYTHS OF THE SELF-TAUGHT DESIGNER

1

THE SELF-TAUGHT ARE A VARIED BUNCH OF RAGTAG
AMATEURS, FAKERS, ENTHUSIASTS, WACKOS, QUACKS,
THIEVES, SIMPLETONS, LIARS, RUBES, CHUCKLEHEADS,
DELUSIONARIES, HOBBYISTS, AND GENIUSES. Beware.

The self-taught arrive on a wave of American optimism that has a wee bit of historical undercurrent. Americans like to believe themselves to be quintessentially self-taught, self-made, self-liberated, self-reliant. We like to believe there is no such thing as social class in America. We like to believe anyone can be anything. We need only opportunity and willpower. America provides the opportunity. The individual provides the will power. And bang! We are who we work hard to become.

This is a hybrid mess of a literary shenanigan, inspired by the dialogues of philosopher Denis Diderot (1713–1784). If you think I took the conversation too far, see Diderot's Jacques the Fatalist (1782).

The myth of the self-taught artisan comprises a subset of the legend of the self-made American. Rules and regulations, certificates and degrees: these replace royalty, title, class distinction. Free us from the arbitrary privileges of birth and class, and liberate us into the great open skies of meritocracy and democracy, capitalism and the competitive marketplace. Smash through the limitations erected by fearful and capricious authorities. Believe in yourself, work hard, and achieve your dreams. Invent a technological wonder. Create a miracle of efficiency. Discover not a new land but a new market. Behold! We are self-made! Only in America!

Bad-mouth the self-taught, the amateurs, the mavericks, the entrepreneurs of this great land of ours, and you're criticizing the promise of America. What are you, unpatriotic? A traitor? You might as well burn the flag.

This is the myth, mind you. This is the opening chapter to the CEO's ghostwritten autobiography. In reality, we live with all kinds of rules. We demand them. As we devise these rules, we argue over whose responsibilities should expand and whose powers should constrict. We have birth certificates, Social Security numbers, high-school diplomas, driver's licenses, passports, voter's registration cards, college degrees, PhDs, JDs, MDs, operating licenses, and board certifications. We have laws, codes, covenants, rules, regulations, permits, and zones. We got it all, from cradle to grave, from head to toe, from bedroom to board room. Let's not belabor the point; let's only acknowledge the complex reality. America has learned the hard way what dangers await us at the mercy of the self-regulated: slavery, monopoly, corruption, the crash of the stock market, and the loss of faith in commerce. Freedom, even market freedom, depends upon the enforcement of rules, or else we are not all of us free.

Has the American All-Star Marching Band of Grandly Sweeping Rhetoric left the building? Yes? Good. Let's narrow the spotlight, dismantle the podium, and quiet the crowd. Let's see who sits at the table. Ah, yes. It's Ego and Devil.

EGO: Hi. I'm a professional designer. I have a degree and several years experience in the field as well as in academia.

DEVIL: I'm Devil.

EGO: Devil? Sure. You mean you're a self-taught designer with no degree and no teaching experience. You have a slipshod portfolio and a part-time job. To compensate for a lack of expertise, you have—Rand help us—enthusiasm. You are an amateur. You do not have the soul of a designer.

DEVIL: I possess the artistic impulse, which depends first on a capacity to destroy and second on a desire to create. To create is to exercise power over oneself and over one's environment. I wish to leave evidence that I existed, that I affected the world in some way. Even a doodle says, "I was," and "I made this." You can choose to be a doctor, but you can't choose to *want* to be a doctor. I could be a doctor and help people, but I would be miserable. I want to make things. I want the power to destroy and to create. I'm Devil.

EGO: I had to go through design school to get my degree. You're a fake. You don't have the chops. You're an imposter. You haven't earned the name.

DEVIL: Design students may also skate by without doing much work. That's true of any student. Grades are the answer to this, but once you have a degree, you've got a degree. Success then depends on luck, networking, will power, and skill. Amateurs may indeed have the chops. What, after all, is the difference between independent work in a school setting and independent work in a home studio? You may be motivated by mentors (professors or online pundits), but in the end we all have to motivate ourselves.

EGO: Maybe there should be a different name then. You can't be a real designer unless you have a design degree. Maybe those with degrees should make degrees more significant.

DEVIL: You already do this to an extent by employment requirements. Academic posts require a degree. Larger firms require degrees, experience, certain skills.

EGO: Then where did these self-taught amateurs come from? How do they survive?

DEVIL: Blame the desktop computer for enabling the amateur designer. Blame the small business for relying on the amateur designer. Blame the market, basically, for creating the technology and the incentives that give rise to the amateur designer.

EGO: Exactly. Amateur designers take work that professionals should be doing, and we'd be doing it better.

DEVIL: Amateur designers often do work that professional designers don't want to do because the work pays peanuts. And, let me tell you, one thing amateur designers struggle to do at this level is to educate these smaller clients about

what design is and why they need it. This is thankless and
unrewarding work. Hours, days, weeks later, the amateur
designer may be left without even a measly business card to
design. Quite frankly, you don't want this heartache. A more
interesting question is how many degreed designers you
need at a particular design firm. Can you get away with hiring nondegreed designers for certain kinds of work? Web
designers must perennially update their skills by attending
the latest software seminars. It's possible firms don't need
that many degreed designers.

EGO: I shouldn't have to compete against those who don't
have to pay off student loans.

DEVIL: Parents can subsidize design students as easily as
design amateurs. Design students who graduate debt-free
are as entitled to their degrees as anyone else.

EGO: But amateurs haven't committed to the craft like we
have. They're just dipping their toes. They're not serious.
They can walk away at any time. They haven't suffered!

DEVIL: You can walk away too. Times are tough. Everyone's
fighting for jobs, especially in the world of graphic design
where expensive print and collateral projects are first on
the block for costcutting. Still, my desire does not depend
on a degree. I wanted to learn design, and I have begun
the long process of self-education (or maybe I should call
it "self-motivated education") and will continue to learn
what I can. The degree is a proxy indicator of commitment
but not the thing itself. Desire, devotion, performance,
production: look to the worker and to the work, not to the
credentials on the door, for evidence of seriousness.

2

At the end of their first conversation, on break in the
hallway, Ego and Devil argue over operative definitions.
Does a paycheck make a professional of an amateur? Does
a seminar make the self-taught taught? For every set of
opposing definitions—self-taught versus educated; amateur
versus professional; self-employed versus employed—Ego

and Devil find exceptions that break the rule. They become mired in concocting definitions based on the reality of what is a pluralistic discipline. Graphic designers range from the teenager given a computer for his birthday to the retired legendary designer with an eponymous academic endowment. Ego and Devil decide to return to their seats onstage and try again.

EGO: The empirical questions drive me crazy.

DEVIL: The biography of any given designer can be deployed to destroy any definition of the profession. If I claim to be an amateur, you disagree because I get paid. If I claim you're not self-taught, you respond that you have to teach yourself every day or else you'd go out of business.

EGO: The variety of graphic designers is why we're coming up with new takes on old categories in the first place. But it's precisely this empirical messiness that can be made to subvert the categories.

DEVIL: There are approximately two hundred and sixty-one thousand practicing graphic designers—one-fourth are self-employed, according to the Bureau of Labor Statistics. They work in print, television, film, digital media, the web. They work for everyone from advertisers to their Uncle Charley's car wash. I want to talk personality, but we end up talking pie charts.

Source for statistics: Bureau of Labor Statistics, U.S. Department of Labor, Occupational Outlook Handbook, 2008–9 Edition. For the section on graphic designers, visit www.bls.gov/oco/ ocos090.htm

EGO: Or self-promotion. The more we defend our own views, the more we appear to be merely preaching what we practice. I claim that designers possess quality X only because I possess quality X. This is a brand of solipsism. The world is the self.

DEVIL: The vocational technician, the entry-level grad, the art-school transfer, the pro-turned-academic, the pragmatic opportunist, the accidental designer—they all justify the terms of their existence by citing the facts of their autobiographies.

EGO: And so all definitions be damned.

DEVIL: Good word choice.

EGO: So what's at stake?

DEVIL: What is at stake and for whom?

EGO: Design schools have their existence at stake. Education is the province of educators. Degrees matter greatly to
those who grant degrees. Credentials matter most to those
who credential. We may impart a cynical motive to these
institutions, but we must also grant them their transformative
role in society. The institutionalized belief in the improvable
individual moves mountains as it moves minds.

DEVIL: I may be self-taught, which requires that I talk to
myself in the corner of an empty classroom, but I'm not
crazy enough to deny the value of the theory of education.
Onward.

EGO: Graphic designers are not regulated by the government. We don't need licenses. The only laws governing our
actions are laws that would govern any employee, freelancer, citizen, etc. We've already discussed the economic
incentives for credentialing.

DEVIL: Credentials serve as proxy symbols of the economic
worth of workers.

EGO: So what is at stake for the employer is the means to
distinguish among candidates. These means may consist of
a candidate's education, experience, skill set, portfolio.

DEVIL: A perspective not to be sneezed at. The employer's,
that is.

EGO: Not least because the employer might also be a
graphic designer who, after years of study and hard work,
moved up the ladder or started the studio that bears his or
her name.

DEVIL: Candidates lacking credentials suffer handicaps
in the eyes of potential employers. The self-taught might,

in self-defense, cite the example of a famous designer who happened to be self-taught. But the fact that some famous designer is self-taught doesn't make your claim to it any more impressive.

EGO: Militias are self-taught. So are squeegee guys and my nephew. Big deal.

DEVIL: Exactly. Okay, so credentials, for better or worse, function for employers as economic symbols. They also function as symbols of social status.

EGO: Social status derives from economic status. Economic signifiers—like education, experience, and employment—become social signifiers.

DEVIL: At a party someone asks, "So, what's your economic signifier?" And you say, "I'm a graphic designer, which, if I'm lucky, signifies about fifty K a year. Who the hell are you?"

EGO: Not a sound networking strategy, I'm afraid. For a designer, parties are not parties. They're work. What is at stake for potential clients, including those you insult at parties, is similar to what is at stake for potential employers, except that employers need only see potential in a portfolio whereas clients want to see fully realized work for past clients. Credentials, like awards, might reassure clients, but the work itself trumps the symbols.

DEVIL: I'd say minimal competence in the work is all that's required before what matters kicks into play: networking, relationships, cronyism, nepotism. And not just between the designer and client but among designers within the same firm. You have to be capable, but like my boss says, the wise old bastard beats the dumb young genius every time. Or something like that.

EGO: So, to sum up, anyone with the intent to design can claim to be a graphic designer in our messy age of design pluralism. You don't need the degree, the tools, the status, the employer, or even a client. You certainly don't need to be good or even competent. You just need the intent. So what is at stake, and for whom, in defining the identity of the designer? Credentials are one way to define identity, and credentials matter to some. They signify to potential employers, signify less to potential clients, and always make our mothers proud. But what is at stake for the individual designer? I think that's where we need to go next.

DEVIL: I agree. Design pluralism recognizes the diversity of individuals working in some measure in a field we've agreed to call graphic design, itself a broad category, its membrane permeable enough to absorb the practitioners of the year's latest digital arts. Together, this pluralism and the attendant technological advances that impact the practice of graphic design disturb the discipline and unsettle the individual designer. In a steady profession and stable economy—

EGO: Both concepts being theoretical—

DEVIL: Many are content to let their jobs define them. Who am I? I am my job. But graphic design is not a steady profession, and the economy is not stable. Uncertainty is the order of the day. Undeterred, people may cling to a mere skill set as an indicator of who they are, defining themselves in narrower and more conditional terms. In a moral panic, a designer might crave the next seminar in web design as if it were a personality upgrade, the next slogan from the best-selling business pundit as if it were a reprieve from a death sentence. Why? Because today's skill set is tomorrow's software template. And today's job is tomorrow's downsized nod to the stockholders.

EGO: So this is why self-definition is so urgent and infuriating. The economic is personal. Who you are today may not even be who you are tomorrow.

DEVIL: I'm an expert in PageMaker. I mean, Quark. Oops, InDesign. Flash. No, wait, I'm a problemsolver! A branding consultant! A, a...

EGO: In this environment, you are not saved by what you know.

DEVIL: What you know is only what you knew. And that's why it feels to me like there is no such thing as art or design, jobs or retirement. There is only the work that you do and the you who is doing it. What is at stake in all this is the individual designer's self-definition.

EGO: And let me guess. What we are dismantling here is the overarching myth of the self-taught, which is that the label of being self-taught no longer functions as a meaningful symbol of the designer's identity, whether as a romantic symbol or a derogatory one. Regarding yourself as self-taught, as a self-motivated learner—as you said before—is becoming an essential component of that self-definition, no matter what kind of graphic designer you are.

DEVIL: Did I say that?

3

Ego and Devil are ready to contemplate the designer's project of self-definition. Ego notes that defining oneself is not the exclusive domain of the self-taught. Every designer enjoys this opportunity. A designer may specialize according to her desire, and this would require rejecting certain kinds of work, whatever their pay scales, in favor of other kinds, whatever their future viabilities. Another designer may simply stick it out in some job indefinitely, accepting without complaint the ebbs and flows of a working life defined by others. The former seizes the day and defines herself as, say, an expert in multicultural branding; the latter suffers quietly and shrugs at the half-finished logo on his monitor. The project of self-definition is as open or closed as any designer wishes to make it.

Interrupting the discussion, a figure emerges from stage right. He flips open a ringing cell phone. Ego and Devil eye him suspiciously. Bald, the stranger wears a purple scarf, cashmere tank top, and jeans. Inky letters squirm on the toes of his spiffy designer bowling shoes. On the left toe is scrawled *Thought*; and on the right, *Trouble*. The stranger speaks.

BUMP: You two are going to be taking calls.

DEVIL: Who are you?

BUMP: I'm Bump.

EGO: As in the bump in our night?

BUMP: As in the bump on your head.

EGO: What's with the words on your shoes, *Thought* and *Trouble*?

BUMP: One always leads to the other, and I need them both to get anywhere.

EGO: So where are we going?

BUMP: Talking about self-definition is fine, but we need a few selves who've done some defining. I'll be cold-calling self-taught designers to hear what these real folks have to say. First up is Bri Tucker of Breez Graphic Design Studio in San Marcos, Texas. Devil in the red t-shirt, you're up.

DEVIL: I think being self-taught matters most to those who are self-taught, and not as a source of shame or a point of pride but as a simple, or complicated, fact. How do you feel about your experience?

BRI TUCKER: Being self-taught felt giddy at first because it was new and fraught with danger for a twenty-one-year-old who was steeped in academics and clutching a newly minted degree in a completely unrelated field. It was a sudden decision to start my own design studio, simultaneously learning graphics software and the complexities of running a business (for which I had no natural aptitude). Pride in being self-taught and self-employed is completely justified. Pridefulness, however, is not. I have humble gratitude that I live in America, where we have the freedom to reinvent our lives, the technology to reach out as far as the imagination can take us, and the luxury of introspection.

DEVIL: The canyons of my ignorance will need to be bridged somehow, and I think the educational experience provides a safe bubble in which, free from the usual daily pressures, you can learn the history of the discipline, the tools of the trade, and the skills of the craft. But I don't want to eat my knees at a tiny desk or be the slow kid in school. But maybe I'll get over this and take some classes. What about you? Will you ever return to school? How do you feel about it?

TUCKER: I will never return to school—not for graphic design. I know I am missing valuable exposure to the history, theory, tools, and skills of our industry; but I am burned out by the demands of academic achievement. I am very good at what I do, and yet without continuing education, I will inevitably fall behind my potential. But while my dedication and joy for making my clients happy is undiminished, I have other interests. My curiosity and passion are now directed toward organic horticulture and ecology. That's right. If I'm ever caught in a class or seminar, or even searching Google, I'll likely be researching plants, birds, or bugs.

BUMP: Thank you, Ms. Tucker. Ego, comments?

EGO: Designers regard design as only one part of their lives, as subplots of their larger life stories, whereas I as a critic tend to look at individual designers as playing small roles in Design's larger story. The eccentric, unpredictable details of any designer's life complicate my wish to present a coherent narrative. I want Design to have a story. Designers want to have lives.

DEVIL: The issue of being self-taught may not matter to Design, but it matters to those who are self-taught. It influences their specific relationship to their work, the way it might for artists and writers and any craftsperson you might name. I'm not talking portfolios, job titles, or industry trends. I'm talking about the personality of the worker, the way a person crafts an identity through their work.

BUMP: The next identity on the line is Brad Jamison of Snavely Associates in State College, Pennsylvania.

DEVIL: Brad, you're a self-taught graphic designer who started out working for a Pennsylvania ad agency. How did you overcome the presumption of ignorance that dogs the self-taught during the interview and hiring process? Was it a smashing portfolio, a willingness to be paid peanuts, or a relative who put in a good word?

BRAD JAMISON: Definitely a willingness to be paid peanuts. My first interview was for a production "artist" job at a publication known for its high turnover and low wages. My ignorance during the interview was probably more obvious than I can recall, but whatever I did worked because I landed the job. Maybe I was the only applicant? My portfolio was nothing special. I majored in Communications in college and had a few projects to show from my one required class. Other than that, I guess it was just good fortune.

DEVIL: How did you think of yourself and your work as you, presumably, struggled to learn and advance in your craft? For example, you might have been insecure as a self-taught designer. So, unwilling to advertise your ignorance of certain matters, you had to learn in secret.

JAMISON: I definitely felt insecure. However, I wasn't afraid to ask questions. I'm sure I asked things that made people think, "What an idiot!" before I finished my sentence. Even so, my goal was to learn as much as I could as fast as I could. My work at first, being primarily small-publication ads, required little design. I really didn't experience design insecurity until I started working for the company I'm with today. That's when it began, that feeling of "What did I get myself into?" It took a long time and a number of projects to overcome this.

DEVIL: You were promoted to senior designer. So somehow you had to improve your design skills and develop your ability to manage other people. How did you do that?

JAMISON: An eyes-open, learn-from-others, spongelike existence was a big part of how I developed. Getting things done obviously helped too. We're a group of fifteen people doing a tremendous amount of work. Everyone wears many hats. My confidence grew slowly out of this environment. A good job here, a happy client there. Acquiring skills was a little different. My creative director mentions often that having an eye for design is not something you learn easily, it's more something that you possess. I spent a tremendous amount of time drawing as a child. I think that a lot of my understanding of basic design principles started with these projects. Software skills came from spending lots of time in front of the screen, reading plenty of tech literature, and not being afraid of trying something new. My company has also provided training opportunities as well.

DEVIL: I can imagine many self-taught designers working in print, crafting logos and brochures, booklets and business cards. But you style yourself an "interactive media expert." This is quite a broad and ambitious bit of self-definition. I am overwhelmed by the Teahupoo-sized waves of media software. I have no idea where to even start. How did you start, and how did you develop your skills to the point where you can bravely stake a claim as an expert?

JAMISON: You are a devil, aren't you? My brave claim comes from our copywriter having a little fun with our website bios. I've learned quite a lot about the, as you say, "Teahupoo waves" of media software primarily though good old-fashioned trial and error. But something too many people lose sight of is that it all boils down to concept and message. I don't know every piece of software on the market. That's not my job. If I don't know it, I find someone who does. Or I bury my nose in another book, message board, or whatever, and solve the problem. So am I an interactive media expert? You make the call.

BUMP: Actually, I'll make the call. Thank you, Mr. Jamison. Next up, freelance designer Chuck Anderson of NoPattern in Grand Rapids, Michigan.

DEVIL: I've read some interviews with you in which your interviewer introduces you as young and self-taught, both of which seem to highlight the fact of your achievements. Identifying you as self-taught implies a certain kind of biography: you're either the intuitive creator, born with a gleam in your eye but no guidebook in your hand, or else you're the heroic loner working hard into the night to learn what you know. What's the truth?

CHUCK ANDERSON: I was born with a gleam in my eye and a passion in my heart to create. I've never really learned anything about art from any teacher or stayed up late at night practicing things. I have always been independent, and in school I was a bit of a loner. I would say I am an intuitive creator who likes to laugh in the face of guidebooks. I'd like to think I'm more of one of the guidebook's authors.

DEVIL: One of the myths of being self-taught is that you lack the capacity to self-correct. You don't know enough history or craft to recognize when you're unintentionally referencing the style of Stalin-era propaganda, rehashing the mannerisms of Modernism, or making every color theorist cringe in agony. To create, you have to be reckless, but to develop your work, you have to criticize it. You have to self-correct. How do you evaluate and develop your work?

ANDERSON: Making color theorists cringe in agony is the last thing in the world I worry about. That's not to say I have the world's best eye for colors, but I could care less what they think about my work if I'm happy and getting paid. Self-correction for me is stopping, getting out of the office and the house, and spending time with my girlfriend or my friends or my family. I don't sit around all day worrying about why the composition on a certain piece didn't turn out right or what I could have done differently with the colors. If I'm not happy with a piece of work, I finish it and say, "Well, that sucked. I guess I'll start over or try something different."

BUMP: That's the beauty of being a designer. We start again. We try something new. We keep working. We mortals can always try again. Up to a point.
And then we can't.

THE NAMES IN THE CASE

AFTER MY MOTHER'S FATHER DIED, FROM COMPLI-
CATIONS AFTER AN ANGIOPLASTY PROCEDURE, I WAS
GIVEN A SMALL SUITCASE, BROWN, SOLID, OLD, WITH
A BUILT-IN LOCK. The case had been my grandmother's.
Many years earlier my grandmother had died from
complications after two brain surgeries. She'd survived the
first surgery and had a hinge put into a cut-out section of
her skull to allow the surgeons access. A year later, in 1980,
the surgeons drained the fluid pressing against her brain.
Postsurgery complications, perhaps a blood clot (there was
no autopsy) killed her. I was ten when she died. When my
grandfather died (in the hospital and, again, without an
autopsy), I was approaching thirty, married, father of two.
I was in the hospital room with my mother and uncle (my
mother's brother-in-law) when we removed my grandfather
from the machines. He defied expectations by breathing on
his own for what felt like days but might not have been more
than an hour. He choked and gasped, unconsciously, until
he lost his strength, suffocated, and died. My mother wept.
My uncle cried. I did not. I'm not sure why. Perhaps I had
made my peace with his life.

    I had come to Chicago on business several times
over the past years and usually arranged a visit with my
grandfather. I'd watched him beat the odds of his physical
health—the consequences of decades of alcohol, red meat,
and cigars—and survive, year after year, but I'd also watched
him decline. I knew that he knew he was living on borrowed
time, because he would tell me as much. He had outlived
his money. He had outlived his desire to live. He would

*Essay on the contents of
a small brown suitcase*

offer me whiskey from nearly clear bottles he'd watered
down to conceal his drinking, and when I would decline, he
would offer me twenty dollars, and I would have to accept or
risk bruising his ego. Then he would tell me that he never
expected to live this long, and I would slip the twenty-
dollar bill into a junk drawer by the kitchen's rotary phone.
He would give me cassette tapes of himself singing, the
nightclub kind of crooning he'd always wanted—but never
had the nerve—to do. He'd never read much I'd written, but
he knew I was a writer, maybe hoped I'd make his life into a
story, real or imagined. I still have the audio tapes he made
for me. And I have the suitcase.

The suitcase tag has my grandmother's name and address
on it. The suitcase is heavy, sturdy, stitched, and reinforced
with some kind of metal in its walls, with rounded rectangular
edges. It resembles a brass musician's instrument case,
vintage, impregnable, something that would withstand the
rigors of life with a touring jazz band or, for that matter, with
my grandfather, who, escaping creditors, moved his family
across the country, from Illinois to Arizona and back again.
My mother and her sister endured different schools every
year. My grandfather had been a Merchant Marine and a
pharmaceutical salesman, but mostly he'd been a bartender
and a violent drunk, disappearing for days or weeks and,
on his brutal returns, scaring his daughters into hiding
beneath their bed. He loved singing "Danny Boy" and sang
for posterity on my wedding video.

A badge bears the manufacturer's name, Skyway, in script
metallic lettering glued beneath the lock on the suitcase. My
grandmother's initials, V. J. Z., are embossed in faded silver
below that. Skyway, founded in 1910, is still in business.

o

CHICAGO POLICE DEPARTMENT

OLLIE H. COTTON
BUREAU OF OPERATIONAL SERVICES
3RD DISTRICT
TACTICAL UNIT

834 E. 75TH STREET   PHONE: 744-8201

---

24 HOUR PHONE
280-9232

DR. DENNIS KERN
SPECIALIST AND SURGEON OF THE FOOT

ROSENBLUM MEDICAL CENTER   LANGLEY MEDICAL CENTER
660 E. 47TH ST., CHICAGO   2117 E. 71ST ST., CHICAGO
TEL: 538-3850   TEL: 493-4500

435-5446 ✓

Edward R. Ward

175 West Jackson Blvd., Suite 303 306
Chicago, Illinois 60604   987-1112

Business: (312) 435-5437
(435-5085)

The ☂ **TRAVELERS Companies**

Representing   Registered Representative of
THE TRAVELERS INSURANCE COMPANIES   TRAVELERS EQUITIES SALES, INC.
Life, Health & Financial Services   Variable Annuities & Mutual Funds

It appears to be a woman's traveling case. On the inner lid are two puffy elastic pockets of the same deep purple material as the lining. These two pockets embrace an otherwise loose, removable cosmetic mirror. An inventory of the odds and ends inside reveals: an old smudged lock, without its key, made by the Independent Lock Company of Fitchburg, Massachusetts; interlocked rings of tarnished keys; the two suitcase keys, miniatures as if for a doll's house, on a safety pin; a cheap glass ashtray rimmed in some thin metal, maybe tin; a stack of unused holiday cards with pink elephants on their covers; five family photographs, in color, including one of my grandfather, myself, and my one-year-old daughter, a photo that memorializes the only time my grandfather ever met one of my kids; a Monaco cigar box of assorted matchbooks, including ones from Full House in Hanover Park, Illinois, Great Godfrey Daniels in Skokie, Illinois, Up Down Tobacco Shop in Chicago, The Parthenon in Chicago's Greektown, and the Playboy Clubs of Buffalo and St. Louis; a strange letter from a family friend or relative; two letters, computer printed and stapled, from the organizer of my grandfather's sixtieth high-school reunion. The organizer typed, to everyone, "I was going to say, 'Be good,' but at your age, I know you are being good," and handwrote to my grandfather, "We missed you. Hang on for our 65th or 62nd!"); and, finally, a small ivory snapshut case, a clock inset atop its lid.

o

Western Pacific Railroad Company
"THE FEATHER RIVER ROUTE"

L. W. (Larry) Leger
Assistant Manager - Service & Equipment

175 West Jackson Blvd., Room 1429
Chicago, IL 60604
Telephone (312) 341-9200
Outside Illinois (800) 621-4466

TERRY'S PARKWOOD INN
3636 WEST 111TH STREET
CHICAGO, ILLINOIS 60655

TERRY COSTELLO
(312) 238-9819

ROBERT B. KRUG

Corporate Insurance Specialists, Inc.
Serving Industry, Commerce, The Individual

PLANNED PROTECTION
CASUALTY AND PROPERTY
LIFE AND GROUP

222 WEST ADAMS STREET
CHICAGO, ILLINOIS 60606
312/641-5660
RES: 312/255-4412

The ivory case with the clock inset on its interior lid appears
to be a jewelry case, or perhaps it is intended to secure the
bedside necessities of a traveler—glasses, earrings, pen,
etc. The case is narrower than a paperback and heavier
than a bible. On the clock's face, which is tinted an ugly,
nostalgic olive gold, is printed, "New Haven." The back
of the clock protrudes into the inner lid. The knobs allow
for winding the clock and adjusting the time, but there is
no wake-up alarm. Inside the case are: cufflinks; a plastic
nametag with Joe, my grandfather's first name, engraved on
it; a black button; two ball bearings; a costume-jewelry pin;
two tiny nuts fallen from the tiny screws securing the clock
to the lid; a black-bead necklace with a cross of Jesus Christ
(my grandmother was Polish Catholic); a nickel-sized pin
from the Chicago Bartenders Union AFL-CIO Local 278 (my
grandfather used to tend bar in the John Hancock building,
among other places); and a haphazard collection of business
cards, collected, presumably, by my grandfather.

o

It is these cards, finally, that interest me most. They suggest
a history of relationships, a past peopled by acquaintances
and friends about whom I know nothing. I never met any
of them. Some may be men my grandfather knew well in
his social circle or briefly, perhaps for a single night, as a
bartender. They are insurance representatives and doctors,
salesmen and relatives. (One card is my own, but I'm not
counting that one.) I have always wanted to somehow
catalog these twenty-seven cards, to arrange them in a
way that suggests an impression of my grandfather's past
or even, I admit it, an evocation of the past in general.
The cards are skeletal and random at best, underequipped
for the documentary task I want to impose upon them.
Still, I record some; what else can I do with them? They
are enclosed inside a case within a case, and no one else
is struck with the impulse to preserve them. Listing
them is a poor substitute for the experience of fingering
through them, one at a time, comparing age and wear, the
typography, the scribbled notes on their white spaces and
backsides. Men handed these cards to my grandfather.

312-252-9268

Nortan's Mens Wear

SPECIALISTS IN TALL AND BIG MEN'S APPAREL

GREGORY METSIG

2959 MILWAUKEE AVENUE
CHICAGO, ILL. 60618

Hozad
674 - 0751

JOHN A. GAUGHAN

PORTABLE TOOL SALES AND SERVICE. INC.
4859 WEST CHICAGO AVENUE
CHICAGO. ILLINOIS 60651   312-379-016

NUMISCO, INC.
RARE COIN DEALERS
NUMISMATIC INVESTMENTS

ERV BESKOW
1423 W. FULLERTON
CHICAGO, IL 60614

312 528-8800
TELEX 25-6219
800 621-1339

Under what circumstances? How many of these men meant something to my grandfather? Are these men—they are invariably men, judging by the names—living or dead? More than a mere twenty-seven men must have handed my grandfather their business cards during his many years as a bartender, let alone his entire life. So why did he keep these particular cards? A couple are obviously the doctors he was seeing at the end of his life. But others are obviously decades old, stained, pocked, torn, as translucent as skin. Look at their jobs, the companies they worked for, their names. What lives did these men lead? How many of them kept my grandfather's card? Did my grandfather even have a card? There is more I can say, but perhaps this catalog and its exegesis only have meaning for me. And what is that meaning anyway? And if I ever define that private meaning in any definite way, how can I convey something of it to anyone else? Most grandsons receive a portion of their grandfather's personal effects, left to them intentionally or, in my case, unintentionally. These are business cards that happened to be in the possession of my grandfather, that happened to be locked in my grandmother's Skyway luggage. These are names in a case, orphans on my doorstep, people from a past that is theirs to know and mine to imagine. It is imagination, I think, that is stirred up by these cards, these bare records of men my grandfather knew. Never intended as epitaphs, they are something else. They are something that makes me heartsick to live only one life, to be denied so much history, to have only one name to give.

ASBESTOS AND INSULATING MATERIALS

GEORGE H. SEVERINGHAUS

GENERAL SALES MANAGER

GRANT WILSON, INC.

141 W. JACKSON BLVD.

CHICAGO 60604

AREA CODE 312

922-8220

NEUROSURGICAL SPECIALISTS, LTD.   (312) 329-1000

EDIR B. SIQUEIRA, M.D.

NEUROLOGICAL SURGERY

530 NORTH

LAKE SHORE DRIVE

CHICAGO, ILLINOIS 60611

Brain Operation June 25 - 1979

SUCCESS YOUR FUTURE!

II

ORIGINALITY

Possible only when you accept and realize your genuine
vocational desires, the nonnegotiable ones that emerge
from the cellar of your authentic self and rudely disrupt
the party of who your friends would prefer you to be

WARNING: A NEW YOU AHEAD!

SUCCESS YOUR FUTURE. How? By using a noun as a verb. This transformation from noun into verb prefigures your personal transformation from passivity into activity. Transform being into becoming. Change your old life of just sitting there like a lump into a new life of running around like a maniac. How? By reading the *Live Well Now! Brainbook* (2009), now with improved identity science.

Live Well Now! is a slogan of affirmation. Live well now, no matter what. It is a hard thing to do in these rough and tumble times. Try anyway. You deserve so much more than other people do. You matter most, much more than most matter.

Live Well Now! is a company that empowers your self-empowerment. Other multinational self-help companies want to help you live your dream. Live Well Now! knows that before you live your dream, you have to dream your life. So sit down, grab your credit card, and check out what Live Well Now! has to offer—seminars, workshops, distance-learning courses, energy drinks, and an official guidebook, or "brainbook."

The following excerpts from the *Live Well Now! Brainbook* include charts, certificates, cards, templates, rules, and a product catalog. Commit to the tenets of identity science contained in the *Live Well Now! Brainbook*, and your life will flow into a future made possible by your giddy self-delusion. But be forewarned. If you don't know who you are when you begin reading this brainbook, you will become someone totally amazing when you finish. Identity science is grammatically awkward but scary effective. And remember: everything is possible to the extent you believe your life is a figure of speech. Good luck.

LIVE WELL NOW! EVOLUTIONARY HISTORY

Species	Date	Dexterity Index
Chimp-hominid ancestor	8-6 million years ago	knuckle-walking, tree-climbing
Ardipithecus ramidus	4.4 million years ago	barely bipedal, stumbling as if drunk
Australopithecus anamensis	4.2-3.9 million years ago	amateur biped, with training heels
Australopithecus afarensis	4-2.5 million years ago	professional biped, still ape faced
Homo habilis	2.3-1.6 million years ago	similar to extras in Planet of the Early Ape Men
Homo erectus	1.9 million to 27,000 years ago	hairy but more human, serious forearms
Archaic Homo sapiens	400,000-100,000 years ago	more modern human, could pass at a medieval festival
Early Homo sapiens	130,000-60,000 years ago	modern but still your basic balcony seat in the hominid theater
Homo sapiens Cro-Magnon	45,000-12,000 years ago	modern human

To appreciate how far we *Homo sapiens* have come in terms of taking control of our instinct matrix and primal skill set and optimizing our creative self-regard, you must understand

OF HOMINID CREATIVE SELF-REGARD

Relationships	Creative Sensibility	Self-regard
clingy	howling	ouch, no, no
clumsy	rock throwing	eat, hide, there
improvised	elevating with branch levers	higher eyes pushing world down hairy feet
promiscuous	repeated vertical hops with limb gesticulation	run, kill, make sharp things
breeding oriented	rudimentary prehunt percussion	take and keep, I get, I have
vigorous but short lived	contemplative rubbing of symmetrical hand axe	me best, you go, you bring me
exploratory, interspecies	rhythmic vocalization during gathering	spin around, dizzy trees, fall down sleep
complacent, multipartner	during storm, gathering in cave, hand-holding, shivering	sky is high, I am nothing
long-term, passionless expedience	cranial self-massage, brow tapping	land is mine, I am everything

where we've been in terms of walking on two legs and making flint tools. Live Well Now! identity scientists present this chart for your evolutionary edification.

$19.^{00} per case of twenty-four (24) 3-oz cans. Warning: not for use by single women at parties. Available free with purchase of week-long Live Well Now! retreats (delivery at the end of the retreat, not at the beginning, for reasons of public safety and mob deterrence).
Product code: O-LWN-83827590

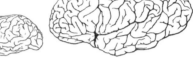

LIVE WELL NOW! BOOST JUICE
Quench your dreams with gusto!
MEGA-THIRST! I.Q. BLAST

$1.^{49} for set of three (3) masks. Not for use at office parties, peace negotiations, divorce proceedings, or in front of children. Flesh-to-flesh adhesion technology activated by body heat and deactivated by meditative brow massage. Not pictured at actual size. Results vary depending on how quickly you remove the mask and apologize. Studies show limited mask duration optimizes viewer relief matrix.
Product code: O-LWN-989893843

LIVE WELL NOW! GLAD MASK
Establish rapport with gusto!
MEGA-FACE! U.R. HAPPY

$19.^{00} per caplet. Daily dosage for adults (18 and older) for effective personality enhancement: 3 caplets/day, with food or liquor. Bulk discount: $12,000/year (regularly $20,805/year). Organic. Nonallergenic. Side effects include run-on sentences, random giggle episodes, nose bleeds, dry gums, aggressive hugging, decreased depth perception, sudden bursts of speed, inflammation of the feet and cheeks, increased sensitivity to gravity, intentional head-butting or leading with the forehead, feelings of self-loss or phantom personality, decreased brain mass, itchy marrow, nostalgia for the future, inability to locate familiar faces in three-dimensional space, paranoia, bankruptcy, voter apathy, shopper's nightmares, reverse erections (downward, not inward), and the monomaniacal desire for the rule of emperor's fiat within single-family dwellings. If staring into space persists for three days, contact a local pharmacist for saline eye drops. May increase frequency of sex drive but decrease duration of specific act (see sexual attention deficit disorder). Reduces acid reflux. Neutralizes fear of growing old. Instills unnameable anxiety. Product code: O-LWN-11012

LIVE WELL NOW! KARIZMA KAP
Bust a Kap in your aspect with gusto!
MEGA-DRUG! Rx SHAZAAM

$9.⁰⁰ Product code: O-LWN-20311948

HOW'S MY
INNER DRIVING?
1-800-GOFKYSLF

LIVE WELL NOW! BUMPER STICKER
Honk if you love gusto!
MEGA-DRIVE! F.U. BEEP

$749.⁰⁰ Purchase of celebrity endorsement includes: one sentence fragment no less than ten words generically positive; one slogan no less than a three-consonant acronym or abbreviation and no more than a two-word sound bite; and one preattached celebrity name with required identifier, e.g., "John Mayer, best-selling author on the U.S. Luge Team" or "Martha Stewart, Emmy Award–winning blues guitarist." Product code: O-LWN-8979902

"Peptastiche!"
—Melanie Griffith, Tony Awards–winning vintner

"Amazoo!"
—Kurt Russell, Vibe Award–winning philologist

"Diqdaq!"
—Alan Greenspan, Golden Globe Award–winning pearl diver

LIVE WELL NOW! ENDORSEMENT
Blurb yourself with gusto!
MEGA-CELEBRITY! V.I.P. HOT

"Floob!"—Jane Curtin, Webby Award-winning chick sexer

$49.⁰⁰ Everyone needs a little squirt… of Personality Gel! Do not apply directly to skin. Don latex gloves, remove cap, squeeze the dissemination tube, and rub hands until you've worked up a lather. Massage gel lather into the countenance of the person you wish to impress. Continue with vigorous massage until their cheeks are ruddy and their brow wrinkles are smooth and relaxed. You should be feeling flushed and pleased with yourself. Remove your gloves with a satisfying snap. Now that's a first impression that lasts! Gloves and matching tights $18.95 extra. Product code: O-LWN-72345809348

LIVE WELL NOW! PERSONALITY GEL
Apply daily with gusto!
MEGA-LUBE! TRAVEL KIT

PERSONALITY ID CARD

Crossing the border into the country of success, you better have your ID card. And when you're set to launch your Effort Rocket into Goal Orbit, refer to the Portable Motivation Booster and deploy with cautious exuberance.

NAME: _____

TYPE: _____

I AM:		I AM NOT:	
	PERSONABLE		TRANSIENT
CONFIDENT	FLEXIBLE	INCOMPETENT	ILL TEMPERED
POWERFUL	LOYAL	DOWDY	FOULMOUTHED
TALENTED	IMAGINATIVE	RECKLESS	NIHILISTIC
BEAUTIFUL	CREATIVE	DOOMED	MERCILESS
SEXY	VIRTUOUS	SHIFTY	IRRESPONSIBLE
STRONG	DEPENDABLE	SUSPICIOUS	LIFE ENDANGERING
LIKABLE	RESOURCEFUL	COWARDLY	REALISTIC
SKILL ENDOWED	LIFE AFFIRMING	BOASTFUL	FUN LOVING

NAME: _____

TYPE: _____

NATURE OF GOAL ORBIT	STATUS: ACHIEVEMENT SATELLITE
1. Captivate an audience of one.	FLAMEOUT, EARTHBOUND, ORBIT
2. Learn a new Photoshop filter.	FLAMEOUT, EARTHBOUND, ORBIT
3. Design a website with sticks.	FLAMEOUT, EARTHBOUND, ORBIT
4. Make your own soap logo.	FLAMEOUT, EARTHBOUND, ORBIT
5. Marry rich.	FLAMEOUT, EARTHBOUND, ORBIT
6. Forgive your guidance counselor.	FLAMEOUT, EARTHBOUND, ORBIT
7. Teach kids to love book covers.	FLAMEOUT, EARTHBOUND, ORBIT
8. God is your client. Surprise Him!	FLAMEOUT, EARTHBOUND, ORBIT

Fill out the ID card with your name and personality type. You don't want to accidentally motivate someone not yourself. Personality types include, but are not limited to: Indulgence Technician, Luck Plumber, Charm Sergeant, Hope Astronaut, Rapture Facilitator, Abundance Millwright, Inspiration Secretary, Creativity Imam, and Shame Entrepreneur. See list at right.

Fill out this side of the card with your name and then also with a record of how well your Portable Motivation Booster boosted your Previsualized Performance Satellite. Circle *Flameout* for total crash-and-burn failure, *Earthbound* for gravity-induced setbacks with possibility of reversal of fortune, or *Orbit* for goal unambiguously achieved.

WHICH PERSONALITY TYPE ARE YOU?

- o INDULGENCE TECHNICIAN troubleshoots cravings.
- o ACHIEVEMENT MIME explores the glass box of a true self.
- o SUCCESS MECHANIC works wonders under the hood of a career.
- o FAITH PILOT radios the big control tower in the sky.
- o GLEE ARCHITECT designs the dreams in the house of the dreamer.
- o CHAKRA COWBOY restores balance to the bucking bronco of self-hate.
- o FLUKE PROPHET foresees happy accidents.
- o IMPLEMENTATION CONCIERGE makes the stay on Earth a productive one.
- o CHARM SERGEANT calls bad manners to attention.
- o PROFIT ANGEL guards monetary earnings with a sword.
- o KISMET NAVIGATOR charts a course for good fortune.
- o HOPE ASTRONAUT space walks on the moon of unreasonable belief.
- o BLISS JOCKEY rides exuberance to the finish line.
- o FATE LANDLORD collects the rent owed to the future.
- o LUCK PLUMBER unclogs life with the snake of positivity.
- o KARMA LOBBYIST puts in a good word in Heaven's Congress.
- o SUPPORT CLOWN distracts the bull of performance anxiety.
- o TRUST GLADIATOR slays the fear of intimacy.
- o AFFECTION METHODOLOGIST sets parameters for relationship dynamics.
- o COMFORT CLERK requisitions warm towels for the lonesome.
- o RAPTURE FACILITATOR books a conference room for ecstacy.
- o CONFIDENCE ELF repairs self-esteem overnight.
- o DESTINY TYMPANIST accompanies the self-realization of others.
- o PERSONALITY STYLIST blow-dries a fashionable identity.
- o APTITUDE FARMER reaps the talent from what nature has sown.
- o WEALTH VINTNER barrels an inheritance.
- o POWER CHEF sautés a reputation in the olive oil of mystery.
- o RELATIONSHIP SAMURAI cuts through the rituals of lovers' quarrels.
- o POSTGRIEF GYMNAST spots the dismount into affirmation.
- o ABUNDANCE MILLWRIGHT fabricates storage units in miserly hearts.
- o DREAM SCULPTOR shapes the night into Giacomettis of waking life.
- o ANTIADVERSITY NEUTRALIZER sweeps the ice for the curling stone of you.

LIVE WELL NOW! CATALOG OF INDEPENDENCE & PROSPERITY

$59.⁰⁰ Personalize a postdated check to yourself to motivate your present self to create a future self who can pay you a lot of money! Product code: O-LWN-20311948

FLIG T. GROMMEL 05-09		**001**
903 Blah Street Nowhere, PU 9834-11	DATE _7/4/2046_	09-77/640 PU 0091
PAY TO THE ORDER OF _Flig T. Grommel_		$ 10,000,000,000⁰⁰
Ten Billion and 00/100		**DOLLARS**
⑈05434328790 ⑆: 000870754" 087908		

LIVE WELL NOW! HORIZON$
Motivate yourself with moolah—& gusto!
MEGA-CHECK! I.O.ME ZIP

$18.⁰⁰ Living well is living right, so say goodbye to righter's block with the Live Well Now! Daily Dice set. Don't want to go to work? Don't want to take the heat for something you did wrong yesterday? Let's face it. It's hard to psyche yourself up when you're sick of motivational affirmations that make too much sense. Now's the time for Daily Dice. With a flick of fate and a roll of superstition, you can change your life for the possibly better. Each side of each die features a word of Live Well Now! positivity. Roll at least three dice, arrange the dice so the face-up words are in a row, and bingo! You've got hope mail! "THINK BIG WISDOM," "FORGE REALITY PEP," and "CHOOSE ECSTATIC LUNG" are some of the insights into the human condition that these dice will reveal unto you. Don't let life roll over you. Use Daily Dice. And roll over your life! Product code: O-LWN-20935793

LIVE WELL NOW! DAILY DICE
Word your fleeting moments with gusto!
MEGA-RANDOM! WORD CUBES

$29.⁰⁰ Available in left- and right-hand puppets. Laboratory tested. Results may vary. Must be 18 or older. Not for use with the Live Well Now! Glad Mask or the Live Well Now! Job-interview Kit. Live Well Now! program sponsors are not liable for damages caused by the use or misuse of this product. Intended for entertainment, recreational, and out-the-car-window purposes only. Scissors not included. Product code: O-LWN-349057280235

LIVE WELL NOW! FINGER PUPPET
Announce your boundaries with gusto!
MEGA-GESTURE! O.K. OFF

$79.^{49} per one-hour treatment.
Product code: O-LWN-23094571

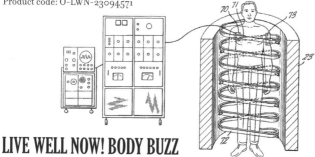

LIVE WELL NOW! BODY BUZZ
Recharge your positivity with gusto!
MEGA-ZAP! +/- HARMONY

If you want that certain *je ne sais quoi*, then all you need is a Live Well Now! *je ne sais* cut! While Live Well Now! products and services remodel your "inner home," let a professional upgrade your curb appeal! Free 10-percent-off coupon good for services at all participating Live Well Now!-endorsed plastic-surgery clinics. Call for details.

10% off OF YOU!

LIVE WELL NOW! CUT COUPON
Slice open your future with gusto!
MEGA-RZR! 10 BLADE

$17.^{00} Worried about your future? Have your palms "red" by the Worry Star! A soothing palm balm for the tense mind, the Worry Star fits as snugly in your hands as Live Well Now! You-niversal Dynamic Systems Thinking fits in your brain. First designed thousands of years ago by da Vinci or Galileo or one of those old guys everyone pretends to know. Therefore, the Worry Star has a proven track record. Some believe the original Worry Star is what gave humans lines in their palms in the first place! Do not squeeze too hard. Product code: O-LWN-911

LIVE WELL NOW! WORRY STAR
Calm yourself with gusto!
MEGA-SQUEEZE! ACU-FUN-CTURE

OFFICIAL SELF-ACCEPTANCE CERTIFICATE

Don't keep yourself in the dark. Accept yourself officially, unequivocally, and in writing. Complete this self-acceptance certificate, and you will enjoy a 100% fixed introductory APR (Acceptance Personality Rating)—at least until a local branch of universal fate terminates the celestial world's acceptance of you.

YOU WANT YOU

LIVE WELL NOW!
Self-Acceptance Certificate

********EVRLSTNG**SXY-01

Step 1

LAST NAME

FIRST NAME

DATE OF SELF-ACCEPTANCE

M M - D D - Y E A R

WITNESS

ANY PREVIOUS EPISODES OF SELF-ACCEPTANCE? Y / N

REASONS WHY PREVIOUS EPISODE/S DIDN'T TAKE:

1.

2.

Step 2

EMAIL ADDRESS

CELL PHONE NUMBER

CREDIT-CARD NUMBER

YES, CALL ME DURING FAMILY TRAGEDIES, INCLUDING DEATH, INJURY, DIVORCE, AND THE SUDDEN ONSET OF VEGETATIVE STATES, TO READ A LIST OF RANDOM WAYS TO IMPROVE MY FINANCIAL WELL-BEING, HABITS OF SELF-STIMULATION, AND/OR COSMIC ATTITUDE.

Step 3

BY SIGNING THIS CERTIFICATE, SIGNATORY OFFICIALLY RESOLVES TO AFFIRM UNEQUIVOCAL ACCEPTANCE OF SELF WHEREOF HE/SHE BODILY INHABITS, AND ALL APPENDAGES, FLAWS, NASTY HABITS, UNPROMPTED CARNAL LUSTS, FATAL MISJUDGMENTS, AND IRREVOCABLE ATTITUDE MUTATIONS (OR "DNA": DAMAGING NEURAL ASSOCIATIONS) THEREOF CONSTITUTING, IN TOTO, THE "SELF" THUS AWARDED WITH ACCEPTANCE BY "SELF" IN QUESTION, MATTERS OF SELF-AUTHENTICATION OF AUTHENTICITY & IDENTITY DUALITY & REGRESSIVE SELF-CONSCIOUSNESS NOTWITHSTANDING, ACCEPTANCE IN FORCE IN PERPETUITY OR UNTIL VACATED BY SUBSEQUENT MISCONDUCT MALCONDUCIVE TO ONGOING STATE OF SELF-ACCEPTANCE, WHEREBY UPON SELF-ASSESSMENT OF SAID MISCONDUCT AND SELF-APPEAL OF SELF-CONCLUSION, THE VALIDITY OF SELF-ACCEPTANCE SHALL BE RENDERED NULL AND VOID, PENDING REVIEW BY SUPREME SELF:

X SIGN HERE

DATE

M M - D D - Y E A R

+ + + **Don't wish your life was better. Bet your life on a wish.** + + +

STLL**HRNY**CLL-ME

U*3V07*1*351073   TNFAD-2009-DB

WON*LLEW*EVIL

DISENGAGEMENT CHARM CARDS

How can you escape politely from someone who is trying to limit your personal opportunity space? Simply hand a disengagement charm card to this person, excuse yourself, and walk quickly toward the nearest exit. Each excuse conveys to any personality criminal that you are committed to pursuing your own self-improvement, not to suffering under their abusive negativity. Try these cards today!

> *I beg your pardon,*
> *but I'm already being fondled…*
> *by possibility!*

> *No, thank you,*
> *I'm already being humiliated…*
> *by empathy!*

> *I'm sorry,*
> *but I'm already infected…*
> *by dream thinking!*

> *I appreciate the effort,*
> *but I'm already being stalked…*
> *by success!*

> *You're sweet, but*
> *I'm already being undermined…*
> *by self-doubt!*

$19.⁰⁰ for a sheet of 50. You may think you're carrying the world on your shoulders, but it's just the duffel bag of your delusion. To celebrate each real or imaginary obstacle you overcome, Live Well Now! offers achievement stickers! Memorialize your minor, if negligible, successes with adhesive circles. If this is the best you can do, then boast while you can. Best results when applied to Live Well Now! Win-the-Human-Race Helmets. Product code: O-LWN-0987345798

LIVE WELL NOW! WIN STICKERS
Stick it to yourself with gusto!
MEGA-GLUE! SKULL STAMPS

Glum? Grim? Grumpy? Great! Answer the casting call for the pilot episode of the upcoming Live Well Now! reality show (working titles: *America's Most Motivated* and *Chump Challenge*). Aspiring contestants on the show must (1) provide evidence of their present "desperate" lack of motivation (e.g., difficulty getting up in the morning, no energy for extramarital affairs, persistent shrugging, the reliance on the retort "Sure, whatever" in response to anything your boss asks you) and (2) demonstrate their capacity for dramatic change in accordance with the script. Must provide 8 x 10 glossy portraits (color, nude). $99 processing fee. Call now.

LIVE WELL NOW! REALITY SHOW
Humiliate yourself in racy situations with gusto!
MEGA-VICE! GROW SHOW

$669.⁰⁰ If ever is heard a discouraging word coming out of your mouth, the Live Well Now! Mood Lifter responds with a quick sizzle to the senses to turn your personal-power outage into a current event. It's shocking what you can do when you let the Mood Lifter keep you motivated twenty-four hours a day. Don't let natural emotional receptivity to social circumstance and the needs of others alter your strategies for enlarging your appetite empires. The Mood Lifter will help you focus on maintaining your opti-growth awake state by replacing your negative verbal expressions with audio playbacks of situation-relevant positivity barks. Celebrity voice-overs $19.95 extra. Product code: O-LWN-11010100101

LIVE WELL NOW! MOOD LIFTER
Watch watt you say… with gusto!
MEGA-SONIC! VOICE JOLT

LIVE WELL NOW! CATALOG OF INDEPENDENCE & PROSPERITY

$187.°° Adopt a pet! This one's name is Opy. He's a cute calf with cyclopia, but don't be fooled. He can see right through your soft exterior to a heart that needs some serious hardening. Pull his monocled spinal cord and listen to Opy the one-eyed cyclops calf say, "Reality is the deformation of our dreams. Deal with it." The natural world is itself a nightmare. And this tragic visionary of a pet needs a home in your heart, soon to be fortified against the inevitability of disappointment. Product code: O-LWN-897025789

LIVE WELL NOW! TRAGIC PETS
Displace your affection with gusto!

MEGA-TOY! CUDDLE BURST

$33.°° Panic can be positive. In this paralyzingly exciting new game by Live Well Now!, players compete to make the most of their anxiety and seizure the day. Up to ten players can participate. Play begins with everyone admitting to the immensity of the world, the vastness of experience, and the brevity of one's time on Earth. Only through generalized observations that confirm debilitating notions can players overwhelm themselves with the limitless possibilities open to them in the game of life. The first player to panic and seize up in a paroxysm of optimism wins the game. Other players engage in pantomiming famous moments of celebrity self-sabotage. Upon completion of the first stage, players pair up with their fail mates and attempt courtship in front of the other players. First couple to succumb to blushing and a panicked retreat to a locked bathroom or closet wins. Product code: O-LWN-908094570-329

LIVE WELL NOW! POSITIVE PANIC
Recognize opportunity—and freak out with gusto!

MEGA-CHOKE! FAIL MATE

The first step in self-renewal is to put your past behind you. But what if a certain someone refuses to keep quiet? Be creative! Neutralize their negativity by sealing them up in the Live Well Now! Move-on Box. Don't just think outside the box. Live outside it. But make sure you hide the box somewhere no one can ever find it. Disposal consultation with unofficial Live Well Now! representative is $499/hour. Discreet delivery. Call from a pay phone for details, pricing, and instruction.

LIVE WELL NOW! MOVE-ON BOX
Move past your past with gusto!

MEGA-LOCK! M.I.A. PRESTO

SPEAKERS FOR ALL OCCASIONS

Office morale in a morass? Don't improve benefits or increase salaries. Instead, put on a show! Call the Live Well Now! Speakers Bureau! We'll send a professional speaker straight to your conference room to wow the workers and motivate the minions. They'll feel empowered without actually being empowered. It's a win/win situation for you and Live Well Now! (and not so much for them). Speaker fees vary according to venue, audience intractability, quality of buffet, relative attractiveness of audience members and waitstaff, open versus cash bar, size of overnight suite, and whether postevent consequences (namely in the parking lot where the speaker rushes past your employees to reach his or her vehicle) require spite fees or gratitude discounts. Placate your peons today!

How OPTI-SOUND POSI-TECHNOLOGY really WORKS!

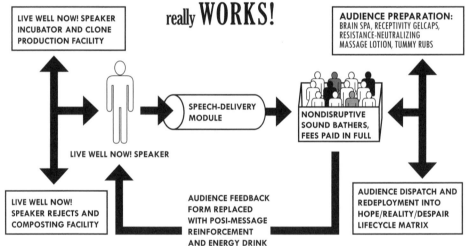

LIVE WELL NOW! SPEAKER INCUBATOR AND CLONE PRODUCTION FACILITY

AUDIENCE PREPARATION: BRAIN SPA, RECEPTIVITY GELCAPS, RESISTANCE-NEUTRALIZING MASSAGE LOTION, TUMMY RUBS

SPEECH-DELIVERY MODULE

NONDISRUPTIVE SOUND BATHERS, FEES PAID IN FULL

LIVE WELL NOW! SPEAKER

LIVE WELL NOW! SPEAKER REJECTS AND COMPOSTING FACILITY

AUDIENCE FEEDBACK FORM REPLACED WITH POSI-MESSAGE REINFORCEMENT AND ENERGY DRINK

AUDIENCE DISPATCH AND REDEPLOYMENT INTO HOPE/REALITY/DESPAIR LIFECYCLE MATRIX

From incarcerated to incasherated, Buck Masters insists that you open your wallet of wealth potential and share your dream denominations with the world. Your spirit of generosity will enrich those standing next to you.

Money Man!

BUCK MASTERS
FINANCIAL FORTUNES

A leading visionary and a spiritual squaw, a mystic of manners and a royal reign in the aspirations, Tabitha Ert is nobody's fool and everybody's guru of go! She'll make you believe you've already done whatever it is you want to do. Voila!

Spirit Woman!

TABITHA ERT
VISION QUEEN

LIVE WELL NOW! HOPE LECTURES
Promise big & don't deliver...with gusto!
MEGA-SHOW! DEMENTERTAINMENT

THE RIGHT PROGRAM FOR YOU

IDENTITY FEATURE	BEFORE LIVE WELL NOW!	AFTER LIVE WELL NOW!	PROGRAM TO MAKE IT HAPPEN
Title on business card	Graphic designer	Dream savior	Half-day seminar ($350)
Job description	Design print materials and websites	Light fires in hearts, open doors to dreams	Full-day seminar ($600)
Shoes	Brown, comfortable, arch supports, thick soles	Shiny black slip-ons of bold walk-on-Evian charisma	Confident Cobbler brochure ($11.95)
Greeting a client	"Hi, yeah, so is your business doing better, or is it still, like…?"	"No, no, your website ideas are very hot. In my mind right now, I'm in a hotel room in Tijuana with your website ideas."	Sexcess Talk Personal Tutoring ($500/night)
Conversational ice breaker	"What's your favorite logo?"	"That one girl from *Sex in the City* chose this shade of pink for her cupcake business."	Niche Cultural Reference Training ($400 subscription to e-newsletter)
Facial expression	Brow furrow and squinting recoil as if smelling foul odor	Pinkie-biting nod with wandering eye scan of person's body	Seduc-Tics: the Science of Reaction Shots ($900/ weekend)
Signature drink	Red Bull smoothie with chai spice and flax seed	Live Well Now! Optimax Boost Juice®	Free case of 24 3-oz cans with purchase of week-long retreat ($3,499)
Theme song	"Shoplifters of the World Unite," by The Smiths (1995)	"Rubbing Victory with the Fingers of Fortitude," by LWN Crew (2009)	*Success Yourself Tonight* ($23.95 CD or MP3 download)
Catchphrase	"That doesn't work for me."	"Let the fame begin."	*You Are Your Own Best Tabloid Reporter and Paparazzo* ($59.95 DVD)
Insult	"Yeah, well, you *should* like white space. Your *brain* is white space."	"Big world, small you, bye bye."	*Continental Philosophy as the Source for Modern Comebacks & Putdowns* ($2.99/podcast)

$29.^{00} Invigorate your romantic life with random acts of uncanny oddness. *Odd Surprise is the New Orgasm* is the new Live Well Now! compendium of sex tips for bringing strange and uncomfortable feelings back into your relationship. In the two-week program, you'll leave a trail of chocolate fetal skunks guiding her to the laundry room where you'll blind her with a handful of sand and cover her with sticky notes. Next, you'll pack a suitcase of her favorite cured meats, pick her up at work in your Segway, and drop her off at the bus station, where she'll enjoy a ride back to work. Keeping your loved one off balance and suspicious is the name of the game. Surprise her with a clean fifty-dollar bill, and squeeze her face. Resolve together to go one day without nagging, and then nag her to orgasm. Put a bathrobe on her backwards, and throw a breakfast of strawberries at her cat. An exciting relationship means never knowing exactly where you stand—or what you're standing in. Product code: O-LWN-69001296

LIVE WELL NOW! STRANGE LOVE
Randomize romance with gusto!
MEGA-SEXY! U.F.ORGASM

$99.^{00} The best way to motivate yourself is to imagine that your life is in critical condition. *Emergency! Hurry! Do something now!* So, if you can't get fired up on your own to do something about your personal and professional failures, let the Live Well Now! Happy Hazard fire you up for real. No flame, no gain. So flame on. And then call 9-won-won to get your life the emergency treatment it so desperately and literally needs. Go on, brush your shoulders off. You're on fire! Happy Hazard product kit comes with incendiary devices, wireless triggers, and pajamas. Product code: O-LWN-929834757

LIVE WELL NOW! HAPPY HAZARD
Combust your complacency with gusto!
MEGA-BURN! 3RD DEGREE

$11,945.^{00} The future you is today's play with the Live Well Now! Dream Doll. Mix a batch of genetic propensities, animal limbs, and pharmaceutical experimentation, and with a little imagination, your physiology can go a long way. So many species, so many recipes, the possibilities are ethically irrelevant and emotionally stimulating. Why wish you could fly when you can implant hawk corneas and surgically attach the wings of a condor? The kit comes with living animal parts, FDA-approved drugs, and a dish of stem cells. Assembled doll is a life-size adult. Product code: O-LWN-77203589

LIVE WELL NOW! DREAM DOLL
The morph, the merrier…with gusto!
MEGA-MODIFICATION! U.S.A. DNA

$51.⁴⁹ Be an active member of the Live Well Now! Ohmland Freedom Force with your very own Live Well Now! Friendly Fines ticketbook. Is someone of indeterminate ethnicity moping around your neighborhood? Is your son's basketball coach negatively influencing the can-do spirit of the second stringers who also deserve playing time in the game of life? If so, then give them a ticket! Fulfill your duty to employ vigilant justice in the Wild West of personality crimes and issue tickets for Negative Thinking, Dream Blocking, Reckless Living, Wish Deferral, Reasonable Goal Setting, Independent Belief System, Sober Worldview, Rational Action, Selfless Imagination, Reflective Judgment, and Being Part of Your Problem. All personality crimes are forwarded to Live Well Now! HQ via wireless transcription transmitter embedded in the paper fibers. LWN! HQ handles all sentencing of personality criminals. Product code: O-LWN-01907457

LIVE WELL NOW! FRIENDLY FINES
Monitor the behavior of others with gusto!
MEGA-COP! PLEASE POLICE

$1,009.⁰⁰ Got a small P.P.? Why your P.P. so tiny? That's P.P., short for Profit Production. With a small P.P., you can't give your customers what they really need. They need it bigger, better, faster, and cheaper. But you have a teeny P.P., and you can't keep it up. To increase customer satisfaction, you need to stick it to them with a big P.P. And to enlarge your P.P., you need the Live Well Now! Opti-Profit Production Plan. With this plan you can maximize your size, engorge your customers, and delight your investors to the hilt. Enlarge your horizon and your circumference. Expect more from yourself and your P.P. You like profit, don't you? So make big P.P. today. And let the money flow like honey. *Yes! Oh, yes!* Product code: O-LWN-9083905790

LIVE WELL NOW! OPTI-PROFIT
Satisfy investors with gusto!
MEGA-MARGIN! Y.U. SO TINY?

$3.⁰⁰ Much more than some banal knockoff wristband, the Live Well Now! Power Collar reminds us that we all belong to something—or someone—greater than ourselves. Take ownership of your insignificance in the eyes of others. Show pride in your solidarity with the superior property rights of those far wealthier than yourself. Opti-Flex-Gro® technology means this collar organically adjusts to snuggle your neck like a naughty noose of obedient love. Comes in Spirit Cloud, Fallen Halo, and Leather or Not. Product code: O-LWN-90174359873

LIVE WELL NOW! POWER COLLAR
Submit to a higher power with gusto!
MEGA-DEFERENCE! U. OWN ME

MOD JOBS

THE FUTURE OF DESIGN WILL BE TO DESIGN OURSELVES. We will modify ourselves for a variety of reasons: to attract lovers, to prevent disease, to live longer. Designing ourselves to this extreme brings up issues of evolution, identity, culture, and power. Through biomodification, pharmaceuticals, and medical techniques, we can change our brains, our bodies, ourselves. We will make sport out of the human condition itself. If we are not afraid of war, we should not be afraid of this enterprise. It is as human as any other.

Physicist Stephen Hawking recommended, a few years ago, that we modify our genome to accelerate human evolution and stop sentient computers from taking over the world. Unfortunately, he said this out loud, and the computers overheard him and have thus accelerated their bid to dominate the planet. Meanwhile, we can't, technically, "evolve" ourselves. Evolution depends on accident; modifying ourselves depends on intention. Evolution takes time; we have no patience. Instead, we would be designing ourselves.

To greater extents every decade, we already modify ourselves. With drugs we modify our immune systems, our behaviors, our moods, calming or arousing ourselves, decreasing our sensations of pain and depression while increasing our abilities to stay awake, concentrate, or run faster. With medical science we are replacing organs, adding new limbs, boosting our breasts, and surgically correcting our vision. We can embed little bits of technology that monitor our vital signs and the whereabouts of our children. Increasingly, computer technology encroaches

Essay on wings, gills, horns, and the inevitable future of design. This essay isn't part of the Live Well Now! Brainbook. I include the essay here because it envisions the future of self-empowerment, and the future is not so far-fetched.

Faster, Evolution, faster!

upon our very bodies, with nanotechnology destined to get under our skin. Extrapolating future modifications is less the province of science-fiction novelists and more the job of entrepreneurs and corporate strategists.

People can get used to almost anything: a clone here, a face transplant there, a dash of stem-cell research, a daily prescription for mood enhancement. Individually, each advancement is no big deal. It makes as much sense to put GPS chips into our children as it does to prescribe them Ritalin or pay for their nose jobs. Surveyed collectively, however, these kinds of advancements seem like a menu for making your own player in a video game, except this time the player is really you.

People will regard their identities as conditional. Minor self-modification drives the health and beauty industries, and it takes only a small leap to imagine major modifications fashioning superathletes, superentertainers, and superworkers. We won't use the prefix *super*—too many negative Nietzschean connotations. But we will confront the prospect of quasi-Darwinian competition in the workplace. We will modify ourselves to work smarter, better, and faster. History is the story of human liberation, and design will take us to a new frontier of liberating ourselves from our very identities. If we can destroy ourselves in war, we can create ourselves in peace (or in pieces). To self-design will be to self-create. New jobs will arise, and modifications will become conditions of employment.

Self-modification will start as tragedy. There will be sad grotesques. But with the tools and the intent, we can design our own personalities. The definition of *human* will expand. Our children's children will look nothing like us. And that will be by design.

Critics will dig in their heels and complain about authoritarian dystopias and corporate enslavement. But science is as unstoppable as profit, and besides, ethics are boring. Just imagine your not-too-distant employment future...

Job: PARCEL CARRIER

Mods: Wings. Eyesight of a hawk. Internal avian clock. Hand scanner. Heat vision enables carrier to tell, without knocking, if anyone is home.

Quote: "My friends who got wings and heat vision now have jobs policing the borders or working for Immigration. Originally, I wanted to be a mercenary, but the doctors screwed up my horn implantation. So now I use my modified moose horns to carry additional parcels. I even deliver in war zones."

Job: ENTERTAINER

Mods: Telekinesis (for entertainment purposes only, by law). Octo-limbs. Time-release biochemicals for on-demand emotions. Specially developed facial muscles for creating the widest variety of expressions—some for the first time in human history. Embedded memory chips save dialogue and screen directions for plays, song lyrics, sheet music, jokes, etc.

Quote: "The trouble with being an entertainer is you're always looking for the next great combination of self-modifications. The audience is fickle. Of course, now with Clean-Sweep technology, I can scan the brain waves of the audience and generate a statistical profile to identify the most appropriate dirty jokes."

Job: MERCENARY

Mods: Exoskeletal armor (a composite of beetle, armadillo, and Kevlar). Paralytic venom cartridges housed in hollow fangs. Organ regeneration. Echolocation for nighttime urban reconnaissance. Neural processors for troubleshooting. Next-generation plastic surgery, combined with computer technology, allows for three facial expressions or personalities: Poise, Threat, and Engage.

Quote: "My flexible armor offers great protection, and although I can roll up to escape, I think it would be just too embarrassing. The best perk is that I can regenerate body parts whether I've been brought down by a bullet, helicopter blade, or even cancer. My body monitor alerts the medical operators back at the base when a tumor, virus, or bullet is doing its damage. Through a wireless connection, the remote operators can locate the offending saboteur quickly, kill it with nano-weapons, and later grow back my liver or whatever."

Job: SPY

Mods: At-will skin camouflage, including environmental mimicry. Optical/audio memory storage and transfer. Foreign-language neural chip. Larynx adjuster (for accents). Follicle accelerator for rapid beard growth.

Quote: "Changing my skin color was intoxicating at first. I changed my skin color in the middle of my first dinner with my girlfriend's parents. I turned blue, then yellow. I went to the bathroom, came out naked, and disappeared into the wallpaper. After a while, they got used to it. They called me the 'Chameleon' and said I should have a sitcom. I actually did want to be an actor, but I discovered I didn't like being laughed at. I saw a D.C. want ad for a modified spy, and the rest, as they say, is classified."

Job: ATHLETE

Mods: Speed of a cheetah. Strength of a bear. Absorption of energy from natural phenomena, such as sunlight, wind, and manure. Subdermally implanted roving massage nanobots. At-will secretion of endorphins, adrenalin, and serotonin for maximum performance. Enlarged cow-muscle-reinforced heart for optimal oxygen uptake. Flex-Bone technology for impact reduction.

Quote: "For energy absorption, I could have had vegetable roots grafted onto my feet, but that was impractical. I chose to implant photovoltaic cells under my skin. My cranial physiometer measures my body status and displays results on an interior optic screen. I can make adjustments in my performance in real time."

Job: AQUATIC RESCUE WORKER

Mods: Gills. Bodysuit made of welded fabric and living shark skin. Second set of clear eyelids. Bioacoustic speech capabilities (including humpback, bottlenose, and killer whale). Retractable dorsal fin and Achilles flippers. Second pair of arms for survivor acquisition and transport.

Quote: "There are different types of rescue workers, each type with different mods. Fire Rescue Workers have lung filters and subdermal coolant. Alpine Rescue Workers have leg extensions and antiavalanche voice enhancement. Because their corporate clients travel, the Elite Life Guardians have both gills and wings, and when they dive into the water, they tuck their wings into back pouches, like kangaroos in reverse. I'm Aquatic, and I got the gills, which are strange and ugly. So I have mine hidden in my armpits. They're special, though. They clean polluted waters as I patrol."

Job: SEX WORKER

Mods: Gynandromorphic gender switching. Variable dermal coloration. Longevity mod turns off the aging chromosome and adds tortoise DNA. Tortoises live over a hundred years, easy. Cosmetic youth preservatives in skin-deep constant-flow wash. Self-defense paralytic-poison-injector nails. Capacity for on-demand limb redundancy (i.e., the generation and manipulation of body parts, like two penises, or larger or smaller breasts). Telepathy-enabled dirty talk. Optional modification for brain expansion to enable simultaneous problem solving on the job.

Quote: "After I became a sex worker, I elected to have my brain expanded. I increased access to the underutilized portions of my brain. I wish I had expanded my brain before I made the rash decision to modify myself into a sex worker, but I guess I needed to be using a greater portion of my brain to figure that out in the first place. So now during down times, I solve global problems. I guess you could say I'm a designer. I'm the one who invented the gills that clean polluted water."

A TRANSITION

THIS CONCLUDES THE LIVE WELL NOW! MATERIALS. It is time for a transition to something new. If the Live Well Now! materials were the result of an exercise in carrying present trends to future extremes, the next section, "The Business of Design," pays homage to an earlier age of career handbooks. The self-help guidebooks of today can trace their roots to Benjamin Franklin's annual *Poor Richard's Almanac*, published for twenty-five years in the 1700s. The career guidebooks of today can trace their roots to books published in the early 1900s in which American optimism found expression in a style that combined sweeping rhetoric with practical advice. "The Business of Design" adopts that style but explodes the form. A contemporary rulebook that breaks the rules, it is a hybrid of advice, fiction, and essay.

THE BUSINESS OF
DESIGN

III

AMBITION

Often confused with a desire to be recognized for doing
something well, ambition is instead a desire to be paid
for doing nothing.

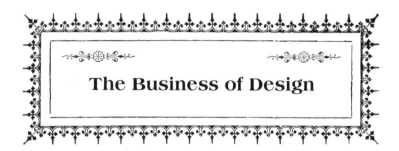

The Business of Design

HOW THE PRESENT WEIGHT AND FUTURE BALANCE OF CIVILIZATION DOES DEPEND UPON IT

SEQUENTIAL CHAPTERS ARE DEVOTED TO THE CATEGORIES OF:
DESIGN, VOCATION, EDUCATION, TRAINING, CHARACTER,
TEMPERAMENT, PENMANSHIP, COUNSEL, PROHIBITIONS,
DEFINITIONS, MATERIALS, GOALS, TESTS, RULES,
MASTERS, COLLABORATION, CLIENTS, TASKS,
LIES, ACCOUNTABILITY, COMPETITION,
CAPITAL, FEARS, FAILURES, FLAM-
MABILITY, DISASTERS, HEROES,
RECOGNITION, GREATNESS,
TRANSFORMATIONS,
SOLITUDE, QUES-
TIONS, & VICES.

Design

Design has in all ages past led the nations onward in the march of civilization. It is a royal leader that conquers the world without staining its hands in human blood. Instead of marking its course with burning villages and smoking cities, as does the demon of art, design leaves behind it booming towns, populous cities, and flowing malls that bear the wealth of millions.

This is the day of the designer. The pioneering spirit rushes into new and unknown media, opens a way through the brambles of raw materials, and fires want into the hearths of the hopeless. The designer clears the view, refigures the wasteland, makes the desert bloom, the mountains yield, and the seas potable.

Who would not be a designer? Who is not?

Without designers the world's civilizations would degenerate and the vulgarities of commerce at its laziest would besmirch the metropolis, inciting the visiting Esquimau, clad in a seal-skin Armani, to remark, "Whose hunting grounds are these?" A city is only a basket, a nation only a stall. Designers woo the goddess of Fortune, and she smiles upon the clerk as well as on the shareholder.

The rocks rising to the temple of Prosperity are hewn by designers into the steps of eternal something something.

Vocation

Thousands leave their homes to seek employment. If they select a pursuit to which they are by nature adapted, they will succeed. If they do not, if they challenge their natural talents and natural natures, they will fail. Let every young person ascertain without resorting to introspection for what labor he or she is best fitted, physically and intellectually, and choose employment accordingly. In the great workshop of the world, there is a place for every designer, but not for every person. Happy is the designer who finds that place and, when the music of destiny stops, sits down first, elbows out.

One is born to build a ship, another to sail it; one to write a book, another to set its type, and still another to misunderstand it; one to design an engine, another to press the ignition; one to steal a patent and accumulate wealth, another to sew up the money bags.

There is a place where every brain and nerve and muscle of the universal body may expend its energy, as the heart of the planet pulsates and throbs somewhere near Wall Street.

Parents, teachers, and the well-established fathers of friends can judge best as to what connections you are, by measure of your society, best positioned to exploit.

What a toilsome voyage do these who merely drift into design begin, rowing against the current of fate. They have neglected duties to corporate entities, arguably. The world is full of these unfortunates. Do not associate with them. Keep your distance, return calls promptly, and learn by their misexample.

Education

Perfection has been attained as never before in the design industry and its sisters, commerce and machinism. Every department of the office of human activity abuzzes with employees eager to make surprising noises and disappear around the corner. Fierce competition! Nerves strain in the perception of distinction!

All departments of industry are subdivided and subsubdivided to such a dizzying extent that baby spiders inhabit the interiors of typewriters, each to a key. Experts, all, in their spheres of influence. Education has been secured as the nominal lever for lifting individuals from the ebb of their idle ways and setting them firmly into the flow of their productive holes. Knowledge is scooping power, and only the educated can pass their tickets to the conductor and have them stamped, officially endorsing their journey on the unwavering tracks of their careers.

To ride such a train, the designer must establish education as the foundation of the construction of his future personhood while monopolies of vast proportions and syndicates of dim stripe assemble to derail competition in its finest whistle and chug. No small matter, this. And this. This, on the other side of the railcar, is the advanced diploma awaiting conveyance into the palm of your educational achievement and, therewith, dissemination, as if casting seeds upon the soil, toward the custodians at the gates of your success. Recognition is your proxy. Beware the urban enchantments. Hasten to know, and know not to question. Fundamental principles include meeting people and elegance of penmanship.

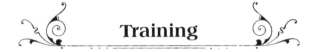

Training

Theory is impractical. It consists, as is generally conceded, of at least 51 percent silt. Theory alone or with a partner does not prepare designers for practical life and the rigors of muscle-based movements. A student designer may master all the textbooks on medicine and law and heraldry and yet be afraid of dark closets of the unkempt. Neither does a course in obstacles pound the necessary decisiveness into the constitution of an under-clerk or cash boy.

Training in practical matters of training, in confidence rooms and business houses, without salary, is essential prior to trafficking in raw experience. Failures are due in large part to the haste with which one undertakes the moment-to-moment embrasure of the open-ended.

A young designer found her seige catapults too weak to properly discharge unto the city of her printed matter, ballistically unfit for the creation and propulsion of the storm clouds of paper she wished to oversweep the avenues and environs, hailing down upon the inhabitants like white wings of gossip. She waited a few months, many things happened, thirteen babies were born before breakfast, and then her catapultment went fine. A lesson in many virtues all at once, indeed!

Character

C haracter is design's soul. It is the measure of the designer's appraisal of the value of other people's wealth, as it
pertains to his acquisition by means of the perception of
the fairness of the exchange of his labor for their wealth. Good
character is like a silver designer. A coin has full weight and
true ring, and a bad designer is a counterfeit of the minds and
hearts of the children of this country, and that country too.

Design is the means to the noble character of the twig as it grows
to a tree, and vice versa. Fundamental business character is no
less honorable than the public-seeming spirit of the million-
aire, each earned dollar a greater blessing to himself than the
blessings of a million of his neighbors or even the neighbors
themselves, weighed in the scale of justice and compound
interest.

Honesty. An honest heart is the noblest work of a designer.
Dishonesty smudges the white space of good credit. Better to
remain indebted to financiers than surrender to the disgrace
of being poor and dirty, in any way. *Diligence.* Work is the curse
of humankind, thus it has consumed the hearts of nations
and the minds of recent graduates and entry-level employees.
One is lost forever, swaying in the hammock of brute minutes
and the moneyed hours. Arise, Pencil and Pen, Mastery and
Machine, and keep time with the mighty revolutions of the
electric things we have to build!

Also, *Perseverence* and *Politeness.* Conquer and be nice.

Temperament

I mpulse is erratic, and the impulsive designer irritable in the itchy sweater of a regulated system. Impulse is tolerable in children, artists, and celebrities, but it is not proper to present gifts of colorful outerwear to serious personalities.

There is a qualitative difference between the hidden urges of adults and the open caprices of children, as there differs in quality the private self-regard of dreamers and the business demeanor of designers.

It is not courageous to stand with the crowd when the crowd stands, to move with the crowd when the crowd moves. It is courageous to stand against the crowd, to move beyond the crowd, and to inflate your lungs with the passions of humanity when you voice a grievance to the custodians of civilization.

Penmanship

L egibility, lightning speed, and beauty. These are the three impossible virtues of excellence in penmanship.

Sit upright, legs relaxed, shod feet on the carpeted or wooden floor. Never slouch or hunch or lean to one side to woo a neighbor.

Your pen or marking tool is not an eel or living worm. It will not wriggle out of your grasp and leave the vented air of the office for the mulch or muck of soil or sea. No pinching.

Move the arm in graceful cadence over the responsive surface, as if conducting an orchestra in the music of foreplay.

Legibility and beauty are qualities dependent on the evaluation of the completed script by an audience or superior. Only the endeavor toward lightning speed can be undertaken and evaluated in the drama of doing. Afterward, there is no evidence of human achievement. It is an original and enduring fact of the designer's professional life that machines can simulate excellence.

Avoid flourishes in business script, unless explicitly requested by the client in a *frottola* or a one-act play.

Practice with head, heart, and hand in synchronous rapture, as if machines had never been invented.

Counsel

Muster courage. Or, if courage lives not within your breast, insert yourself into circumstances that will reveal a silhouette of imitation courage while you are safe to keep doing what you always do.

A career is a niche for an imitative species.

Look on the bright side of things, by which repeating of this counsel is also a way of looking on the bright side of things. Meanwhile, get up early, work hard, go to bed late, and don't get sick.

A clever designer shall stand behind kings, lewdly gesturing to the crowds during festivals, such as the Festival of the Non-Defeat Aspiration, the Festival of the Groomed Flaw, the Festival of the Doctored View, the Festival of the Prurient Peek, and the Festival of the New Show in Town.

Accrue to your own account the pleasures of a life lived, and never mark these accounts to a journal, unless you are sure it won't be found.

Strangers make the best customers.

Inflate your reputation with preemptive self-advertisement.

False flattery is the child of a smug heart.

It would be nice if you need never call any designer master. Be tactfully self-reliant, and call your master by his honorific or use a nickname, which is dangerous water, indeed.

Pride of creation does not translate to pride of acquisition or pride of ownership. Designers, do not mistake pride in the excellence of your craft as communicable stuff. Your clients will not share your pride, for they have not done the work. Creators they are not, in this relationship. They are purchasers of value, acquirers of mood. Designers appreciate their past as proof of their current self-worth. Clients invest in the future in hopes of potential aggrandizement.

If you know the value of a dollar, you will know how important it is to find more.

If a client has withheld a small amount of money, and it cannot be collected without recourse to lawsuit, you should drop the matter and consider it a lesson in prudence, unless you know a thug, and then the client should learn the lesson.

Design the circumstances for breaking a heart and accept the nausea of responsibility.

The alphabet of success consists of twenty-six elements and of these are seven virtues, three talents, two capacities, five skills, four insider recommendations, eight favors, one witty remark, three manipulations, six deceptions, four or five white lies, several acts of expedience, one well-armored ego, thirteen compromises, thirty-one compliments extended gratuitously to superiors, very little math—which can be delegated—and, finally, luck, fortune, fate, destiny, chance, and the devil's grudging kiss on the cheek as you leave your doorstep for the rude wide world of human affairs.

Prohibitions

Never be a nut without a kernel. Empty form will not conceal the ugliness of vanity. Never wait for chance to come to you. Wait for it to come to someone near you, and take that one.

Never design if you would rather move mountains.

Never accept help when you can get paid for doing it yourself.

Never compete against a superior designer's manifest skill. Hire her for it.

Do not be distracted by the look and feel of money, else you leave yourself without the means to make it. Focus, rather, on the designs at hand, and trust no one.

Never eat cake while you still earn rice.

Never lose an opportunity to state your name, describe your business, and explain why you are the right designer for any job anyone can think of at that moment.

Never shovel coal into a steam engine when you can feed hay to horses.

Never be civil to those who don't deserve it, especially when witnesses are liable to record your insincerity.

Never promise to complete work at a certain time without being sure the client will believe your future excuses.

Never trust a vendor claiming to sell at cost.

Do not accept advice as a map behind your eyes. Do not let others drive your thoughts. Rather, spread their advice on a table, in quietude, and study its wrinkles, contours, and latitudes. The map of their advice has borders. The table has an edge. Stand above these representations of the bordered world and awaken to your own masterful perspective. Most people don't know what they're talking about.

Avoid speculation for worry's sake. Invest in the strategy of your own gain. Save for the inevitable betrayal by close allies and banks.

Never forget that if you appear faithful to your friends and family, you will have forgiveness forever.

Never give a client your home address.

Definitions

Quality of life depends on quality of mind, which depends on quality of language. Heightened experience requires both practiced sensory perception and the vocabulary with which to render its significance to yourself and others.

To convey impressions of your own experience to others, you are often bound to language as the flatbed truck for that conveyance, even when your experience is not linguistic or textual but visual, auditory, tactile, and olfactory.

To savor experience you must define experience, and definitions involve the abuse of words.

It is for future designers to convey odors that summarize a poem, sounds that describe the texture of a touch, and images that define an odor.

To enhance your perception, you must exercise your imagination. Expand the control room of your mind to include maps of the surrounding dimensions of experience, as measured and reduced by sight, sound, smell, touch, etc. Construct these maps in leisure, with fine concentration, to guide your judgments in times of haste and fury.

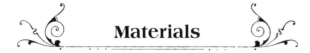

Materials

L ife is too vague a material to work on with any success. This
is a mystery. Squishiness is a sensation one feels between
the toes when standing in the sinking mud of eternity's
rising tide, gasping for the air of something more to be said,
intelligently, about this mystery.

Materials can include an object that provides a bumping interaction within a frame of reference, or an idea that threatens to
cause a concussive effect within a population of rival groups.

Life is often cited as source material for creative works, although
life has never been footnoted with precision.

Materials can include things discarded, disorderly things making
themselves orderly, broken pieces of mismemory, light.

Life is filtered through the lenses of human experience, that is,
seen and sniffed and felt, a hand running up the inside of the
thigh of Experience. This filtration residue is rendered by a
variety of crafts into bits and threads and buttons of flesh and
packed into the whole of a creative work, submitted then for
judgment as to cohesion and coherence and the potential for
comic energy. The sticky photons of life are bent in the perceptions of the mind and deflected onto recording devices. The
world, framed, is chopped into perspectives, the designer's
body interposed between perceptive mind and thrashing
world, tempting disappointment, courting an oblivious lover.

Goals

The majestic and minor goals of design are:

To enter by objective proxy–art and made thing–into another's impression of the world.

To press the small of the viewer's back and gently, gently...

To hold a face in your hands and wait.

To ask, "What do you...? Would you rather...?"

To dare to suggest that this here now is all there is of this here now.

To accept the limits of media only at the time of fabrication within that media and, upon completion, to let your mind off the leash and wander into the dark woods beyond the lamplights of polite behavior.

To smuggle news of the world into the minds of loners.

To smuggle news of the heart into chambers of prejudice.

To whisper lies into the ears of your enemies' friends.

To propose that the opposite proposition is never the only other proposition.

To alert the senses to their functions.

To exercise the thinking mind, to add connections among the floating butterflies of neurons, to associate enemy with friend, like with unlike, the things of the world with the things of the mind, thoughts in one department of the brain with memories in another, law with sweater vests, history with furniture, empire with cargo, to speak to the inner voices of the silent and brooding and barely hopeful.

To mate the gesture with the feeling that gives rise to it.

To express in the open what lies dormant in dream.

To swim in the spongy matter of the brain, the flooded house of our minds. Thoughts are structure, encoded fiber and drywall, pipe and wire. Reach them, connect and disconnect, and in any way make a means for the residence of the new.

To sell real estate in the city of people's more pressing concerns.

To disrupt the narrative of another life.

To grab the collar and pick the pocket of daydream, and display the goods in the tears of sunshine.

To snare a glance from the dull and dulled.

To sing in the auditorium of the otherwise unmoved.

To surprise with the nervy sizzle of a sneeze.

To sear the fat off assumptions.

To create an utterance that creates its utterer.

To snuggle in bed with another, flesh to flesh, skin to skin, the comfort and terror of being together, which reminds you that at all other times you are alone—and to be conscious of having had that thought while being together, an unshared thought and memory of prior loneliness, summoned into the skin of the now in which you are also alone, despite, despite, dammit, and even, and no matter what, the terror of being within yourself and trapped, a coffin of skin, the consciousness of a match head, struck.

Tests

The tests of a design are to be described objectively and applied subjectively, as according to the spirit of the self-appointed judge, in keeping with the seemingly arbitrary nature of existence and the entertainment value of the indifference of fate. Tests are to the designer what sidewalks are to the hands and knees of falling children.

There are at least seven known tests for design. The Appearance test examines color, luster, shape, and intentional and unintentional marks. The Chip test evaluates the ductility and lasting taste of a chip flaked off an edge of the design. The Fracture test submits the design to sonic pulses in order to hear cries of brittleness, reports of grain structure, and pleadings for mercy. The Magnetism test is self-explanatory. No design has ever survived the Melting test. The Ring test involves striking the design with an iron church bell and recording the fertility rates of brides. The Spark test deploys a grind wheel to reveal the design's spark volume and pattern of spark branching.

Designers, be forewarned. Imagine the distinct form of your yet-unmade thing. Imagine it in the flux of its context, moving in space and time, abrading the surfaces of other lives and apparitions, flitting wings. See your bone gleaming in a desert of apathy. See your shapen object tip on the windowsill of What Is, crushing the skull of What Was Previously Minding Its Own Business. What have you done? Glimpse your fatal consequence, retreat in horror, surrender to faith, and pay.

If it exists, what is not useful?

If it dies, what is useful?

Rules

1. Designers, during work hours, attend only to design matters.

2. No designer will be successful who neglects the visual clarity of the highway code and the raucous birds of beauty flushed from the tall grass of daily life.

3. Honorable designers respect the images of words over words about images of words, although excitement can be found elsewhere.

4. Make your intent known to your audience of one or one hundred with sharpness of manner and visibility of the apparatus of timely appeal, such as a suggestion box or whim bin.

5. Cut your losses. Tighten your pucker. Be firm yet dry in your embrace of the warm bodies of young trends.

6. Alert your conscience to the affairs of your unspeakables. Withhold judgment of your behavior even though you would judge others the more harshly in the expiation of your shame.

7. Settle arguments swiftly, compromising only with labor, never with discounts. Hold grudges lightly, as weapons for tomorrow's negotiations, and keep accurate accounts of your lover's whereabouts during the workday.

8. Sell hops to brewers and grass to goats. Accept the world.

9. Never qualify your endorsements of your designs. Never.

10. Value your work highly; never bargain with deal-hunters.

Masters

Designers, like newborns, believe the world to be unexplored, undiminished from its original state, as freshly slick with the juices of birth as themselves. The tests of life and loss, however, have smothered entire populations as callously as urban landlords refusing to adequately ventilate multifamily dwellings sealed in the heat of August. Like all before them, designers will have masters.

Before any young designer are arrayed twelve body tubes of employment opportunities, eleven of which are filled in with cement—courtesy of the departments of highways and human resources—and sealed with the tacky plastic film of top-down policy changes. Life perpetuates itself, thanks to carbon chemistry, the double helix of deoxyribonucleic acid, and competition from international industries. From their parents, children inherit characteristics—including mutations, such as physical deformities, lust, and criminal tendencies, as well as virtues, such as a strong back, the ability to nod indefinitely, and a natural inclination to allow self-interest to wither into a vestigial virtue, as useless as stubborn desire. Masters are necessary and need no more justification.

The qualities most esteemed in masters of design are somewhere to be found along the meridian of happenstance and the coast of charity, but these qualities are rare and flightless and do not often survive the migration to the mainland, where, for reasons known to private bondholders, more hardy creatures predominate. Masters survive by adapting to weather conditions not over time as a species but in the moment, quickly, slipping into galoshes in the foyer and, meeting the storm in the street, popping open umbrellas. Masters are practical beasts with no sympathy for wishful thinkers or weathermen.

Profit crowns the innovator. Masters take charge of higher hills whereupon new shapes can be discerned in the distance, new routes blazed along the horizon of possibility, new secret deals hidden in the gullies this side of the cliffs of bankruptcy. Hitch your wagon to a master of this rank, and you will ride safely on a journey of sheltered convenience until, beneath the canopy of your servitude, you will be afforded a view of the master pulling farther ahead in another wagon that you had not noticed during the prior years of your faithful employment. You were too distracted in your loyalty to figure out what the bastard was doing. He saved himself by keeping his eyes on the prosecution of his own pointless progress. What have you done for your loved ones? Profit is a fickle priestess. She goes not to the earnestly employed and melodramatically submissive. Don't you see the time you have wasted posing for Mindless Trust and Devotion? Profit will not be courted but by the devious lovers concealed in the crowd.

Keep in mind the dynamic between designer and master. A designer toils in the shadow of a master like a child cowering in a closet in the home of new foster parents. Designers should always accept the master's suggestion for improving the design and make the change swiftly and in silence, like drawing a dagger across a throat.

Collaboration

A great many designers are destitute of employment for months on end. A wise designer conceals his financial reality with simple, elegant clothes purchased from franchise outlets, and while he cannot afford a home or a horse, he indulges in smaller luxuries for reason of psychological consolation. He consumes exotic libations publicly, whereby he triples the enjoyment: his vanity is soothed, his social worth is advertised, and his mental state is overthrown by the coup d'etat of caffeine, alcohol, sugar, or the collective conspiracy of all three. On the street and in this unbalanced condition, a designer is likely to meet a colleague. In such artificially convivial circumstances are collaborations conceived.

If the weather is cold, the two might share the chores of cutting firewood, stoking a fire, running back out to a street corner to sell surplus artifacts, using that paltry sum to purchase the little comforts of snuff, tobacco, spirits, or the services of a dance instructor. The designer on the errand returns with the acquisitions to his collaborator, to whom, by firelight, he introduces the dance instructor. A feeling arises that dance has been, somehow, the reason for this assembly from the start. The trio hazards a step or two, the twin collaborators mutely obedient and timidly deferent to the dance instructor. In an inspired moment, one of them notes the absence of melody and hastily equips the atmosphere with the vibrations of recorded fantasies, as achieved by instruments wielded by the skilled hands of dead musicians. The significance of art and mortality is lost on the three of them, intellectually, while their primitive vitality sings with emotional urgency. They dance to the miracle of music until evening. They sup. Having supped, they ride in a cariole, boisterous at midnight in the bracing snow. They return within the hour, healthy and robust. They do not desire rest. They are intoxicated with wakeful consciousness, the glory of being. Urged by necessity, capable of enduring patiently the greatest exertions, they *collaborate for hours* until they are eventually sapped of strength. Naturally lively and heedless, they exult in having overreached in this affair, and they sink into slack appearances, as if aging a hundred years during the epic descent of their heads to the pillows. They sleep until daylight.

The cigarette ash is cold. The plastic audio disc revolves tediously. Songbirds beak the sills. Snow piled high to a gentle mound suggests only a memory of the form of the cariole. In the early afternoon, the dance instructor opens her studio. The two designers shuffle to town and split up to look for real jobs.

Clients

In ancient domestic life, the client ruled as absolute monarch over the designer. So it is still in emerging countries. Mature civilization has softened this. Laws regulate the relationship between client and designer. As long as the designer waits for payment, he or she is subject to the control of the client, who has all reasonable authority to enforce obedience. As long as a designer is properly treated by the client, no one has the right to interfere or assist the designer to escape if this were against the wishes of the client.

Clients have rights to punish their designers, so long as the punishment is not cruel or videotaped. Surveillance video and photographs of brutality are punishable as crimes because recordings are objects rather than people and thus easier to imprison in a locked bottom drawer. The acts of punishment depicted in such media recordings are typically submitted as supporting material for television writers pitching new programs. Clients are well advised to "correct" their misbehaving designers in the dark and leave no bruises.

While the designer is employed, the client has a right to all work product, including whispered insults and wisecracks, which may be repurposed as slogans for new products.

A designer has no right to leave the workplace without permission from the client. If he or she does, he or she may be brought back to the workplace by force. Force may include physical capture by netting or hook, as well as psychological capture by shaming techniques or telemarketing. Designers often return on their own for reasons of poverty and boredom.

Tasks

Design is a directive from the governing class of a country to its inhabitants telling them what they must or must not do, how they must or must not do it, and what expressions are appropriate for the occasion. Every civilized nation has a system of design, and no nation could exist without a system of design stolen in part from somewhere else.

The nature of commerce compels designers of different lands to adopt shared customs for prosecuting matters of business. Designers and clients and representatives and citizens of all lands must reach agreements, and someone has to make copies of all that paperwork. Much needed, too, are closets and filing cabinets and fireproof safes.

Business relationships invariably depend upon social relationships. Designers must task themselves with the intricate dynamics of social entertainment. In eating and drinking, go to excess. Eat everything set before you with voracious and indiscriminating appetite. Run a wooden spit through a shank or leg, hold it over a brisk fire until fur or feather is burnt off, and seize upon the roast with the teeth, working the jaw. Suck fermented liquids through straws to increase aeration of the liquor and rapidity of inebriation. Take great pleasure in dancing. Dress fancifully while shuffling in the midst of elders, who sit and smoke. Rhythm is critical. Harmony is optional. The atmosphere will devolve into a tribal approximation in which coconuts are offered to evil spirits at dawn, worthless to stall the inevitable approach of man-made calamities.

Lies

Lies do enhance and maintain the rotation of the social sphere of polite commerce. One can wield truth as a weapon of spite and vengeance. Lives are wrecked on the shores of truth. *What do others think of me? Have I honored my mother? Am I satisfying the fashions of the day?* Indeed, truth brushes the tiger's fur the wrong way. Lies calm the hackles and cushion the blows of experience. Lies invigorate the entrepreneurial imagination and reassure the tourists. Amen.

What are some examples of lies? They are: observations too new to verify; the results of early exit polls; the delivered message wherein she promises to write as soon as she arrives on the opposite side of the world; that educational loans are easily repaid; the claim that the termites will leave the crawlspace under the house and the mold will dry up in the walls and flake to nothing; that what is owed is the same as what is hoped; that there is glory in tumult; the insistence that fidelity to fidelity is courage; that friends remember what you did for them; the promises made by cops and council members, brokers and bartenders, candidates and lovers; that deferred hope is ever recoverable in its original intensity; that forgiveness is due to the old merely because they have grown old; the faith that the fallen curtain of your first life on Earth will rise, and you will once again take the stage.

Accountability

Those who would hold designers accountable for the consequences of their designs are polite, modest, civil, indolent, spiteful, wily, and fastened like molded grips to the paddles of ancient prejudices. They should as soon hold planetary bodies accountable for the consequences of gravity and chide the moon for its lack of ambition. Design is a natural force of humanity, despite its definition.

The great scolds insist on accountability for all but themselves, for the review of all judgments but their own, for the remedy of all consequences but theirs upon culture. They enjoy contentment of mind and vacuity of personality. They are as untempted by compassion and complexity as they are devoted to simplicity and sobriety. Their clothes lack any ornament and deter any interest. They must secure spouses by secret arrangement and the threat of rumor. To their credit they construct their own homes and furnish them with the handmade semblances of chairs and tables, which by their blunt surfaces and stiff lines do punish the eye as much as the seat. Their principle article of food consists of pea soup over boiled pork. They drink sour milk and rum, often separately. They greet all—strangers, visitors, family, and friends—with equal candor and attentiveness, that is to say, falsely. They have much to conceal and wish to invite no suspicions that won't ultimately prove true. They present an appearance manufactured to please, and you will scratch your head for days, in your jail cell, wondering who among them put you there. Indeed, it could be any. It could be all.

The cautionary tale of design accountability turns on the fate of a musician's wife. The musician, from a defect in his parents and a preference in his tongue, contracted a youthful fondness for spirits, one which, his doctors advised, would be the death of him were he not already dying of mortality. He took their advice and instead wandered his hometown streets in despair and sobriety for six weeks, bothering shopkeepers, leaving his sheet music to the goats and his piano to the dust mites, and nearly bankrupting the tavern owner.

One day he saw the pale countenance of a young woman reflected in the tavern window. He felt no tug at his heart to compose a melody, as was often his urge when beauty surprised him. For a month she returned to show her face in the glass. It felt like a month to him, but it was only an afternoon during which the lady shopped on the main street and the musician, sober into his seventh week, slouched farther down to the pavement. The musician at last gave a prophecy. He foretold of her eventual infidelity to the man she loved. The young woman thought quickly and bought the musician a drink.

The musician regarded her arrival into his life as a castaway regards the mirage of a ship. He composed fiendishly, always with a bottle before him and his wife behind him. Yes, they married, and years later, as he was to perform a classic piece to win a university post, he altered sections of the score so as to send a secret love note to his wife in the audience, who was sure to notice. She did, and scolded him, even after he won the post, for she was not impressed by the public nature of the expression. She was also upset at being left alone during his prison sentence of six months, meted out for altering the classic score written by the deceased grandfather of the university president. The president was intolerant of disrespect. While a classic scold, he was an effective fundraiser.

The musician was, indeed, held accountable, though his wife forgave him. They had seven children. The couple was forever faithful to each other, disproving the musician's early prophecy, which was only one of thousands of the musician's absurd rantings the wife promptly dismissed, counteracted, or consigned to history. In such ways are the misfit products of creative genius best dealt with. It is a lesson for the scolds.

The musican's wife died, paralyzing the musician in grief. He never composed, drank, or visited a doctor again. Mortality was not to be trusted. As an affliction of humanity, the musician thought, mortality was faithless, unpredictable, mysterious. His wife had left him for death. Who was to blame? He starved himself so that his children could outlive him. They did.

Competition

Not until our modern political economy accepted the
dynamic of competition could it vie with the opulence
and productivity of ancient civilizations ruled by
pharoahs and kings and emperors, manipulated by corrupt
and greedy priests and merchants, and built and maintained
by slaves, prisoners, and the poor. The town hall depends for
its spiritual legitimacy on the church or temple down the road.
Golden feathers frame constitutions. See the courthouse, the
orphan and foundling hospital, and the colleges of grammar,
philosophy, theology, and war. Touch the gilded edifices of
beautiful white stone. A fine powder whitens the lines of your
fingerprints. Lick the dust of eons from your fingertips, and
tongue the grains of art into a dissolving paste. Clouds float
on their backs through the serene pool of the sky. Appreciate
the broad avenue, the trees sheltering the arcade, porticos
delicately vined, footpaths winding voluptuously into the
intimacies of alleys and gardens, the air tinged with baking
bread and beignets. A parrot speaks in dialect from within
the drooping bough of an orange tree stationed outside of
an emporium, luring customers with sensual riddles and
promises of rapture. Deep within the bosom of history, you are
intoxicated with the perfume of powder and flower petal, dizzy
with the ecstacy of a transported soul, in love with a generous
vision of the world cupped in the palms of your expansive self-
consciousness.

Competition is the buttermilk lotion soothing the rough hands
of people forced to live together. Civilization depends upon
its designers to apply this lotion, to rub it in, and to smooth
the exchanges of relative value among the desperate and
fearful inhabitants of society. Designers are indispensable
dispensers of the competitive spirit of commerce, good will,
and virtuous restraint. Reality is sensual. Designers direct the
senses toward isolated encounters, the experience intensified

for being selective, narrowed, essential. Designers may distract the intellect, even unintentionally, but more so they direct the focus of sensory organs, the eye, ear, finger, and tongue.

Competition is the pounding rhythm of the heartbeat writ large into the body of the populace. Today is the day because today is always the only day. Let no one forget this. Let no one sit idle in ignorance of this. Let no one be dismissed by history for want of the direction of a designer. The experience of moment and moment and this moment, too, can be distilled into a focused essence, a narrowed consciousness of emotional time, the sensual anatomical apparatus of each individual employed to suck deeply from glittering fountains of created wealth and flowing value. Competition is a singular aspect of our time, integral to the health of a society but consisting of only one perspective on our modern human condition. Our condition is too beautifully complex for a summary reading. Yet designers hark to the beat that resounds in their bodies. Competition is the urgent thump of a living universe.

Capital

Capital is a fat, unctuous substance prepared from the cream of human labor by means of agitation, separation, and isolation. Within its economic system, capital is synonymous with other concepts within other economic systems—such as wealth, oil, equity, piety, surplus, honor, bounty, treasure, bonus, extras, goodies, reserves, caches, potential energy, and the oxygen in the atmosphere of human interaction. When pure, capital is soft, malleable, soothing, and of an agreeable, sweet taste. Its features include limitless transferability and shocking ethereality. Any individual recognized legally as "human" can serve as owner of capital, though any other individual, even one not recognized legally as "human," such as pirates, slaves, mercenaries, nation-states, nomadic tribes, animals, natural disasters, and corporations, can acquire it, steal it, appropriate it, abscond with it, deplete it, disperse it, bury it, hide it, give it away, waste it, invest it, gamble with it, burn it, tax it, drown it, and in other ways diminish it to the very millionth of a fraction of its existence and then, with a flick of the eyelash, extinguish it. When capital is kept for too long, it acquires a peculiar smell and taste known as rancidity. Ingenious machinery of private and public concoction exists to reintroduce stale capital into fresh vessels for transportation into the veins and arteries of the economic body. Capital disintegrates into lesser elements but retains the potential to be reorganized, recombined, and refigured back into the hands of the few. There, it is resurrected as capital once again. Blessed are the designers, for they shall rarely grease their lips with the true fat of capital.

Fears

The intensity of the love of life relates to the intensity of the fear of death. Vitality relates to mortality. Depression is deep because of this fear. Passion is high because of this fear. A maker's moods are moved by these undercurrents, these great deep bodies of emotion whose heaves and lulls can be read on the surface in calm and in storm.

Irreverence and recklessness—the characteristics of a designer at play, one who expresses a love of life in the desperation to engage with life. This designer indulges uninhibited gestures of form, heedless of moral duties to self-correct. This designer risks the humiliation of error and trespasses against fear of self, moves beyond the preemptive naysaying of forseeable shame. This designer secures by odd means a partial vista onto someone else's experience and transforms this vista into an objective doohickey. From cooking to serving, this fool paces, paces, with reddened ears and scuffing heels, paces in the back kitchen while strangers chew at his lopsided heart.

Fear your lazy whims. Fear your preference for the familiar how-to program for life, never seized upon and modified by personal digestion but, rather, passively accepted and discharged, the way a voyeur accepts a view and turns, turns to accept any other.

It's the punch you don't see coming that teaches you how to see.

Failures

The common failures of designers consist of:

The choice of advisor to whom to lend credence.

The choice of career to fall back on.

Lack of principle and overzealousness to compromise, even in fees and in marriage.

Willingness to be late in arrival and late in departure, first and last only with a show of disrespect.

Stupidity of aspect and visage.

Laxity of conviction.

The easily uncoiling feline purr expressing your dependence on the stroke of flattery and the caress of compliment for your reward in this life and the next.

Surrendering to habitual methods of satisfying base urges.

The distractions of obedience and the policing of sins.

Faith in surgery for the restoration of moral courage.

Praising insufficiently the sacrifice of mothers.

Denying envy its due.

Too little deference to the healing regimen of waiting for the possibilities of next week.

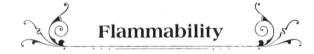

Flammability

Fire is a prevalent disorder in Design, as well as in the adjoining province of Property. Upon attaining a certain magnitude, a fire indicates a state of emergency. People beset by panic are not uncommon in the vicinity of fire. There are different gradations of flame-induced panic, and various causes have been assigned for this phenomenon as it occurs within the neighborhoods of Design. One observer blames confined air and its stifling effect in the employment sector. Another observer speculates that fire is a consequence of bad water or the absence of water or a population of dry people, insufficiently moistened. Irrigation from a swampy tract and many basins carried from a mineral spring offer meliorative remedies, though there is little hope for their application in the real world of flammability.

Inhabitants of a flammable district or township enjoy good health and meet with few accidents, other than the fires.

In a fire or other emergency, designers can be counted on for presuming the haughtiness of another needed expertise, such as medicine. To cure the sting of a scorpion or centipede is commonly required. In a fire, creatures retreat and seek safety in burrows or in distance established between themselves and disaster. Panicking residents leave home without footwear and in stepping heedlessly impose their soles upon another being that in reflex defends itself with nature's instruments of tooth, claw, beak, stinger, or scent pouch. To soothe stings, one may tug at the lower jaw of a small fish until the jaw is torn away, whereupon the horseshoe-shaped jaw is set around the stung flesh, and the rows of needle-sharp teeth are hammered into the swelling area until it bleeds freely, flushing the poison in a cascading flow. The jaw is removed, the toxic blood is absorbed with cotton or linen and tossed into the approaching fire, and cool succulent leaves are wrapped and bound over the wound.

If the fire was caused by lack of water, small fish are unlikely to be found, and succulent leaves are likely to be rare, if not burnt to ash. An alternative remedy resorts to the use of actual needles and sterile bandages. Needles may be disinfected by passing them through nearby flame. The designer may opt for bandages and ribbon or a belt to secure the improvised bind.

Property is flammable. Property consists of art, tools, furniture, books, pajamas, bicycles, homes, and other objects fabricated by human wills and ways out of the wealth of the planet. It is a testament to the human imagination that elements of human anatomy are also subject to isolation, categorization, manipulation, and intellectual-property rights. Property must be designed, unless property were rocks or dirt, although even rocks and dirt may be designed, fabricated, polished, distributed, and advertised as "natural" and "flame-resistant." Designers embrace the business of making things and must accept the limitations of material things, most notably their flammability. People and property, beware. Design burns.

Disasters

A single-celled organism can be killed by an asteroid hitting the planet's surface, punching a crater a thousand feet across and sending plumes of ash into the sky as high as mountains; but at the same time, a common bacteria could completely occupy a planet the size of Earth in a few days or weeks under suitable conditions. And so an alien microorganism frozen in space ice could, in the impact with Earth, be dislodged from the asteroid, come to rest on a sunny glade, and emerge from the chilly pool alive, intact, and mobile, swimming beneath a scrim of ash on the surface of a river, on its way to infect the creatures of our world with a fatal disease from outer space. Life is unpredictable.

Design, like all disciplines and vague terms of art encompassing the entire goals and strategies of a devastatingly consumptive species, is subject to a long list of disasters, most of which the natural world has yet to unleash and a few of which humans will inevitably unleash on themselves via the poisoned fruits of technological progress or the simple mechanism of male stupidity. Design can be victim of flatness, dullness, ethereality, irrelevance, invisibility, disposability, flammability, whimsy, obsolescence, melting, asteroids, disease, an epidemic of poor judgment, and spontaneous disappearance, such as being abandoned on public transportation or floating away on a small raft or inflatable device.

People too often respond to the destruction resulting from disaster with the creation of delusion. The disaster destroys. That is all—no more and no less. Disaster is often defined by the extreme of its consequences as much as by the nature of its means. A breeze refreshes sunbathers on a hot summer's day while a tornado threatens to splinter barns and heave portable dwelling units into ravines. But the tornado does not rise to the level of disaster unless it actually destroys a barn or portable dwelling unit. Achieving destruction, the event achieves status as a disaster, but its meaning ends there. Its story is complete. Survivors of disaster seek to expand the meaning of *disaster*, to enlist its depleted force into service as an activating trigger for whatever may come next into the lives of the survivors. Those who suffer and fail blame the disaster. Those who overcome and succeed credit the disaster. Both endow the disaster with an animism, a spirit of intention, to create a personal relationship where only a temporal relationship exists. The individual and the disaster spent time together, shared space together, and that is all. All else is myth.

A young man contracted a drowsy disease and, in the quietude of his home recovery, discovered the joys of reading books, sketching birds alighting on branches outside his window, and folding paper into sculptures of fanciful architecture. Later in life he credited his drowsy disease as the cause of his career as a designer. Had he not contracted the disease, he argued, he would not have had the opportunities to read books, sketch birds, or fold paper. Had he not contracted the disease, he argued, he would not have had the opportunity to be alone with his thoughts, to explore his desires, to realize his talents. Had he not contracted the disease, he argued, he would not have become a young man able to sit at home and look around him and consider his prospects in the world. The drowsy disease made all that possible. The drowsy disease gave him life itself. Had he not contracted the disease, he argued, he would not have become a designer.

The successful designer helped to found a new design school. The first course for first-year students was Introduction to Design. Why was it not Contraction of the Drowsy Disease? Certainly, young designers would do well to contract the drowsy disease as quickly as possible, and preferably within a design school outfitted with windows overlooking trees favored by birds and stocked with graphite pencils and folding paper. But even the designer did not believe what he claimed. He simply preferred the self-aggrandizing myth, the one in which his strength was proved by a trial of martyrdom, his success owed not to the will of vanity or the juices of desire but to the virus of fate and the charity of disease.

Disasters, like designs, come in all forms, and the hardest to control are those we imagine.

Heroes

She pushed the eye farther back into the head, made seeing an act of bodily resistance rather than a vessel for reflected light.

His ego was too big for his body of work.

He was young and asked too many goddamn questions.

She was eager, quiet, and spread the disease of looking askance.

He felt embarrassed surrendering to the structural dynamics of his five limbs.

She cupped darkness in the river at night. At dawn, she let the paper absorb the stain.

He was pretentious, but at six years old, he still had time.

He set true gems against the not-nothing of white.

She set counterfeits amongst a tangle of ornament, ornament that by her alchemy became the gem.

Recognition

Recognition arrives packed in crates of all sorts, sizes, and smells. Crates rarely arrive on the doorsteps of designers, or perhaps today they arrive with increasing regularity, morsels inciting the appetite of the ego by which strategy designers are tricked into working harder without proportional compensation. The Market is at work in boots and a clipboard. Designers see a tuxedo and a microphone.

From each crate emanates a seductive patter. Recognition whispers your name. It surprises you to hear it. You listen and are transfixed in the posture of a moron. Fame is a value any idiot can recognize. The rough-hewn crates tickle the fingertips, the alien whispers resound as a lover's song, and you never pause to sniff and identify the odors curling through the seams.

Like fuel in the dead of winter, you are a scarce and expensive article to the family freezing in the hut of your soul. Take care of yourself. Manage your natural resources. Panic, and frostbite mortifies the flesh. Master yourself, and the climate of your mind will become salubrious and fertile. In profusion will you produce flowers, myrtles, oleanders, walnuts, figs, pomegranates, apricots, almonds, lemons, citrons, olives, grapes, melons, and cucumbers. You must esteem your personality. You must appreciate fully its inherent value.

Let no one manipulate you with fear. Others may remind you of the consequences of disobedience, which may include humiliation, loss of reputation, and physical distress. These are simply other words for death and its cousins. Let your capitulation be revealed, and you will be humiliated. Let your compromise be recorded, and you will lose your reputation. Let your complicity in the soiling of your integrity be written as a newspaper headline, and you will suffer a physical distress.

Death is not a power others hold over you. Death is natural, inevitable, and inescapable. Those who would manipulate you cannot promise to extend your life beyond death. With what, then, do they threaten? With fear. Fear is also natural, inevitable, and inescapable. So do not believe anyone can relieve you of it. Manipulators cannot keep even that promise, for it is by keeping you afraid that they achieve their advantage.

Yet they promise victory, success, immortality, and truth. Surrender to the promise of victory, and you lose. Surrender to the promise of success, and you fail. Surrender to the promise of immortality, and you die. Surrender to the promise of truth, and you lie. For if you surrender, you no longer exist. You have become someone else, someone who does not deserve these rewards. And who will be first to remind you of your loss, your fall from grace, your victimhood? Your conquerer, at every turn, will remind you that you are a slave, and that fault lies not with the conquerer but with the conquered. He will insist that you have enslaved yourself. And you will surrender to this argument because surrender has now become a habit with you. It is what you know best. It is safety without freedom, comfort without pleasure. You sought recognition. And no one recognizes you.

Recognition earned by corrupted work cannot bestow nobility. You were already noble.

Greatness

Great designers die like the rest. A single design may earn the designer recognition, and subsequent designs may combine into handfuls that may be packed into a reputation, visible as adjectives or references within the print or ephemeral media. This recognition lasts for a time. Then greatness ends, without ceremony, without fuss. Those who appreciate greatness identify not with the great but with visions of themselves as great. A great designer's life provides an entertainment in which the viewer substitutes himself in the lead role. The viewer dresses up in the cape and boots of that designer's style and pretends to endure the adoration of the public, of which, ironically, the viewer is a part. He thus adores himself, playing all parts in a costume farce of vanity. It is a banal convention, then, that the viewer murders the great designer and takes his place in order to experience the entertainment. A great designer is both the god and the sacrifice. At the conclusion of that entertainment, the viewer seeks another entertainment in which to play the lead role—to murder a god, assume the power, and bask in the envy. A great designer is not a person. A great designer is a chance to dream.

Transformations

A designer may live quietly, below the surface of noise and notoriety, in the happy mud of work and fellowship. A designer's greatest design may be the creation and development of her own personality.

She starts with only the raw material of the self, with urges leaking out of neural containers, social impulses evolving out of proportion, fears and anxieties out of joint and wreaking havoc in the larger mechanism of consciousness. Engaging the tribe or social unit, eating meals with family members, giggling at bodily eruptions, wiping blood from a corner of another's mouth, the raw consciousness accepts the anchors of the material world and draws the first wires of self taut. The mind accepts the evidence of the body's senses, that there is a world beyond the skin of her own existence, and she yields to the tension of the wires as they draw her into encounters with nature and humanity, with trees and clouds and younger brothers. Her self rises to meet her senses, and experience is created of this collaboration between subjectivity and objectivity, between mind and material, fingers breaking the warm crust and dipping into the boiling fruit of the pie. She screams with joy.

She learns and grows into someone larger. At night, her dreaming mind reviews the day's events, refiring the neurons in and out of sequence, while the sleeping dog at her bedside jerks its legs as it, too, chases the day's rabbits this way and that. She intends, she acts, experience happens, and her sensory life encodes a story, submitted for elucidation in the imagination. She wants, tries, feels, thinks, dreams, and makes memories as she makes new selves.

She discovers a means of engagement with the world that rewards her as no other. It is a particular category of work. Work is one

name for what humans do to the world. She finds that breaking things into smaller things and using those smaller things
to make bigger things is a thing she loves. The wires stretching
between herself and the material world tighten and vibrate.
They sing. Sensory information flows as intention flows as
action and reaction flow between the things of the world and
the churning operations of her growing mind.

History describes the movements of populations and the judgments of kings, the eruptions of volcanoes and the decimations
of wars, but it offers literature as the means to understand the
relationship of humanity to the material world, that is, the
relationship of the species to its work. Science today scrambles
to peer into the working mind. Science knows there is an epic
story of transformation told within the drama of an individual
seeing someone else reach out for a glass jar, of imagining what
it would be like to reach out for a glass jar, of forming the intention to reach out for a glass jar, of reaching out with one's arm
deployed in motion toward the glass jar located in space and
time by the surveillance of the eye and the intelligence of the
mind, of seizing the jar, and of squeezing it until it shatters
into glass dust and a thousand brilliant fragments.

The individual was a watcher until, by thinking about what she
was watching, the individual transformed into an imitator.

She reviews the fragments, arranges them, sorts them, frowns and
messes them up, cutting a laceration into the palm, crosswise.
She reaches out for other objects. The epic drama repeats with
variation, layered upon the previous epic dramas of intention
and action and assimilation.

The individual was an imitator until, by thinking about what she
was imitating, the individual transformed into a creator.

She imagines a figure. She imagines a thing of many parts made to resemble an imaginary version of something real or something new or something that vibrates. She presses the fragments into this thing. She makes it bigger, chunk by chunk, pushing it, pressing it, until she has made it newly whole.

These epic dramas repeat with variation, layering, relayering, connecting, reconnecting, vibrating, continuously represented in the mind, subject to the deformations and reformations of the imagination, while she grows in time and place, becoming a designer, the raw material of her embodied humanity transformed over time into a unique, vibrant, working personality. The designer becomes a personality new and surprising and welcome, but she is alone and contained within a shape of mortality and lost, today and forever, to us.

Solitude

Joy of working blesses few, intensely and fleeting. Joy of working is rare, valuable, addictively self-reinforcing. Awake and safe at home, well-fed in fitted forms of loose cotton, alone in a bath of windowed sunlight, the designer creates and in the doing converses with himself. Somehow the designer surprises himself with the creation, having concocted the means to surprise himself more than the means to make the thing idealized in the mind. That is, he planned the action but accepted a variety of outcomes, accepted that those outcomes could not be planned definitively to arise from a series of actions. Mistakes can be designed. Errors can be planned. In the conversation with himself, the designer describes the process of making, the feeling of making, the trials and errors and near misses of making, reports to himself as if he were both a designer working in this room and also a child listening in another room, peeking around the corner and stifling a yawn or a giggle. "Do that again!" the child says, and then later, "Do something else."

Where is the place in the brain for creating? The brain doesn't apportion its tasks so discretely. It is not a factory or beehive, computer or office building. It is an organ of electric liquidity, a humid inner space of frenzied improvisation. Most parts communicate with most other parts. It is an open system with itself and its senses, limited but capable of adaptation and imagination, endowed with spindle cells, mirror neurons, and a love that transcends neurotransmitters—yet susceptible to injury, mutation, and the sway of cults.

What is the evolutionary explanation for the desire to surprise ourselves with our made things? There is value in creation—in design and work and crafting a horseshoe or catapult—as there is utility in the consequence. But emotion reinforces the working, some emotion connected to pleasure, pride, ownership, consciousness, personality, and the vital shock of this crude evidence of our own existence. Made things represent the growth of ourselves, even as the making of them influences that growth. Solitude is a fact of our being. Work proves the existence of consciousness. Made things warn others. We are alive and alone, and we are dangerous.

Questions

What is the difference between *making fun of* and *having fun with?*

Is your work about things or is it about people?

What is an eye, that bulb rooted in the soil of the brain?

What is an ear, that wrinkled pit of a drum room?

What is a nose, that two-way tunnel to the lungs?

What is a mouth, that nimble sphincter of sound?

What is a hand, that articulate insect of greed?

Is your work about bringing things to people or bringing people to things?

Is your work about putting things inside people or putting people inside things?

With all the light from the billions and billions of stars in the universe, why is space so mostly dark?

Where do you live that is so immune to oblivion?

Isn't it nice that *loess* is another word for *windblown dust?*

Do you have much time left?

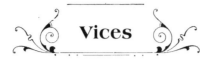

Vices

H abits of mind start with naked first efforts, well before habit has a name.

Pages do not turn according to the nature of books but according to the customs of readers.

Media do not operate according to their natures but according to the customs of users.

Linearity of narrative is a tribute to the autocracy of Time, appeal to any higher dimension being unlawful.

Beauty is mostly pretty and a little ugly, in honor of humanity and in respect of the democracy of grace.

THE HIND PARTS

IV

CHAOS

True chaos will never be perceived by organisms because
organisms are orderly. You can't even dream of chaos.
Even dreams have order.

GUIDE FOR READING THIS BOOK

Some parts may need to be read twice.

THE NINE EMOTIONS OF THE WORKING DESIGNER, BY CHRONOLOGY

1.   VAIN SELF-PROMOTION: *I can do anything!*

2.   SELF-DOUBTING HUMILITY: *I undervalue myself and submit a low bid for a design project.*

3.   RELIEF: *It's the first thing I feel on winning the bid, as if I didn't deserve it or someone's doing me a favor.*

4.   GRATEFUL ACQUIESCENCE: *Grateful for the chance to work, I acquiesce to whatever extra tasks they ask for, including multiple long drives to meetings, any and all changes— three versions, expensive proofs, etc.*

5.   EXASPERATION: *Fatigue sets in, and I succumb to the weaker emotions of resentment, spite, and righteous flares of self-esteem, all too little, too late. I should exercise, eat better, and learn something from the experience, but instead I work to Public Enemy, Ministry, Fugazi, and Rage Against the Machine.*

6.   REGRET: *I regret I didn't charge more.*

7.   RELIEF, PART II: *The first thing I feel on getting paid. I feel relief that money still exists (it's been a while since I've seen it in person) and for receiving the money without (much of) a fight.*

8.   DENIAL: *With money finally in hand, does anyone believe they have been fairly compensated? Up close everything looks smaller, especially money. This is counter to the laws of perspective—closer is bigger—but in line with the laws of desire and gratification—wanting is big, having is small. I ignore the disappointment and move on.*

9.   VAIN SELF-DELUSION: *I can do anything!*

HOW TO INTERVIEW FOR A JOB

o Anticipate the interviewer's questions.

o Prepare your own questions.

o Never interview with a company unless you sincerely want to work there. Declining offers indiscriminately demonstrates bad faith, and you will encounter some of these people in professional life.

o Practice interviewing with friends and relatives.

o Know the employer. Research the company's history, staff, clients, and any citations in the news.

o Know the answers to typical questions.

Why do you want to be a designer?
Find a vivid, concise way of making the point, such as an anecdote about a role model, school experience, or work experience.

Why do you want to work for a small/medium/large company?
Emphasize the advantages of the size of the company. Do not disparage other sizes of companies.

Why do you want to work for us?
Be specific. Do the research on the company.

Why do you want to work in this geographic region?
They want to know you're going to be there a while. Cite some prior connection to the area, such as growing up there, family ties, or past employment.

What are your hobbies or interests?
Do not talk more passionately about your hobbies than design, because they will screen you out. Be reserved and characterize your hobbies as marginal to your central devotion to a design career.

What are your design-related strengths and weaknesses?
Emphasize the strengths relevant to the fields in
which the company operates. Do not admit your true
weaknesses. Instead, name a general area, such as
writing, speaking, or historical knowledge, in which
you are striving for a high level of excellence by, say,
studying great writers, orators, or historical figures.

o Early in the interview, establish a connection between
you and the interviewer based on mutual interest or
experience. Prepare questions on design, an alma mater,
professional associations, clients, hobbies, or children.

o Know the answer to any question you ask the interviewer.
You don't want to make the interviewer uncomfortable or
defensive. Prepare questions on your potential duties,
possible training, the company's clients, the company's
culture, and public service.

o The successful interviewee is rational, not enthusiastic;
is attentive, not relaxed; speaks concisely and only when
necessary; gets the interviewer to talk the majority of
the time; asks at least one prepared question based on a
mutual interest or experience; asks at least two questions
about the company; does not jump to conclusions; and is
not overly critical.

o Respond to a tough question by asking a clarifying
question or by describing how you would go about
researching the issue.

o Respond to negative questions with short, unemotional
answers. Never volunteer or admit to unflattering
information about yourself.

o Respond to an extended silence by asking a prepared
question.

o Lunch, dinner, and casual interviews are dangerous.
Interviewers want you to let down your guard so they can
find reasons to reject you. Don't drink. Don't order what
anyone else orders. Don't tell personal stories. Don't

discuss controversies. Be sociable and reserved. Observe how they behave and ask yourself whether or not this company is right for you.

o Let the interviewer end the interview. Compliment the company. Say you would love to be a part of it.

o Send a thank-you note, but keep it short and professional. Mention a common interest or topic to remind them of who you are. Don't ever try to fix a broken interview. Learn your lessons for the next interview.

A COLLAGE OF COUNSEL

Ask yourself whether your style is appropriate. We need it to be innovative and done quickly. All attempts seen so far are way off base. I get a lot of stuff that is way off track—aliens, guys with heads cut off, etc.

Send samples that tell a story (even if there is no story). We purchase fine art for the covers, not graphic art. Those who require high fees are wasting their time. The economy has drastically affected our budgets. We're looking for a humorous take on business. Be innovative, push the creativity, understand the business rationale and accept technology. Pays for design by the hour, $15-25.

Be willing to change midcourse. Be willing to accept low fees. Be willing to have finished work rejected. Our readership enjoys our warm, friendly approach. These are tough times. Pays for design by the hour, $10-20. Relax and enjoy the adventure of being creative.

We are not interested in working with artists who can't take direction. I like to be surprised by the artist. Say you'll keep in touch and do it! And please don't call asking if we have any work for you. Don't give up!

Freelancers must understand design is a business.

We don't pay contributors.

Please, no aliens or unicorns. Be familiar with our publication. Familiarize yourself with our magazine. Be very familiar with the magazine and our mission. Please see our magazine. Please read our magazine. Review our magazine. Have a look at the magazine. We suggest you review recent back issues. Call me and tell me you've seen recent issues and how close your work is to some of the pieces in the magazine. Read our magazine. Check out our website. Take a look at the magazine (on our website).

Let the work speak for itself. Assignments awarded on lowest bid. We are actively seeking new ideas and fresh humor. I would like to have more artists available who are willing to accept our small payment. Give us a try! We're small but nice. Do not say, "I can do anything." You are only as good as your weakest piece. Be yourself. No phonies. We are starving for satire on the human condition.

We like to look at everything.

This is a collage of excerpts from the 2006 Artist's & Graphic Designer's Market. The excerpts are taken from the Tips sections of the Magazine category and the Advertising, Design, and Related Markets category. Magazine editors and company representatives provide these tips to graphic designers looking to submit work. They are intended to be helpful.

THANKS

Thanks, Mom.

QUOTATIONS

"It is compassion rather than the principle of justice which
can guard us against being unjust to our fellow men."
— Eric Hoffer, *The Passionate State of Mind* (1954)

"If the basic principle of collage is the juxtaposition of unlike
things within a visual field ... [Robert Rauschenberg] need
in theory only find stranger and stranger things.... The
theory ... ignores the true source of this artist's power,
which lies in the mystery of particular choices."
— Donald Barthelme, *Not-knowing* (1997)

THE NECESSITY OF OBJECTS

Little projects tempt me to distraction. An essay here, a
photo book there. The kids and I make collages. We cut
up magazines, catalogs, newspapers, and old books. We
hunt for books at secondhand sales and library giveaways.
We arrange our clippings on notebook pages, sketchpad
pages, or posterboard. We print out our emails and paste
them into the collages. We draw words and doodles in the
spaces between images. The kids tack the posters on their
bedroom walls. The bliss of small achievements is fleeting
but real. Rarely can you point to something and say, "I
made that," and then offer it to friends for inspection and
confirmation. So sometimes a small object is necessary.
An artist once explained to me that he painted a crushed
pop can in the foreground of his painting to "hold down
space." I think small achievements are like that, solid
imperfections that hold down the space of our lives. They
are functional, like good shoes.

THE SYMBIOTIC LIFE CYCLE OF BOOKS AND PEOPLE

GLOSSARY

Aesthetics | the philosophical equivalent of having someone else's nightmare.

Amateur | one reckless enough to risk being interesting.

Art | the form by which we come to empathize with a created self.

Audience | doesn't know what it wants but knows what it's afraid of.

Art | what the audience is afraid of.

Beauty | the quality one cites in self-defense when caught liking something too much.

Celebrity | the only fascinating way to be boring.

Content | what the brokenhearted settle for.

Creativity | to be blessed with the capacity to haunt oneself and cursed with the incapacity to pacify one's fear.

Critics | cheerleaders for a team that never plays.

Ethics | to have them is to be in possession of stolen goods no fence can sell.

Form | what is essential to art and bureaucracy.

Function | a delusion: everything is always something else, and something else is always what we need.

Genius | term of endearment for a misbehaving puppy.

Imagination | the capacity to construct artificial worlds.

Knowledge | what we barely remember about what we almost perceived.

Light | what we take to be evidence of solar energy makes our own beliefs visible.

Madness | a formlessness of mind.

Morality | a group license to frown upon what an individual has achieved that the group could not.

Movement | a refinement of one or two inclinations of the previous movement and a loud disingenuous rejection of all others.

Posterity | a lie; to be flawed and forgotten is the fate of all works and all makers.

Pretty | what a tourist concludes upon looking out the window of the bus.

Professional | one skilled in the tedium of excellence.

Reality | what no one understands and everyone complains about.

Religion | what artists accept when immortality refuses to accept them.

Reviews | why waste time interpreting the art that is when you can review the art that isn't?

Sanity | the maintenance of the appearance of that which has something to do with neurons, chemicals, and the capacity to hold a job.

Self-criticism | the only criticism you won't be arrested for.

Space | only one organ of a larger organism.

Style | to create a style is to bring a simulacrum of a personality to life; to maintain a style is to love a corpse.

Survival | so ancient a concept, its enactment must be televised to be made real.

Talent | observed in lazy children by their mothers.

Utility | is all that's left when we've fallen out of love.

Work | what makes dying alone feel like living with friends.

INTERVIEW CREDITS

In all cases in this book where a quote is not accompanied by a citation, the source is an interview with the subject conducted by the author. The author interviews of the subjects are quoted in the following essays: "Evologo," "汉字 Welcome," "Red & Yellow Kills a Fellow," "Left Wanting," "Danger Muse," and "Myths of the Self-Taught Designer."

PUBLICATION CREDITS

Some work in this book appeared in edited versions in *I.D.*, AIGA's *Voice, Eye, Opium Magazine,* and *Hobart.* "Evologo," under the name "Raining on Evolution's Parade," and "PAR͜ADISE," under the name "Pharm Team," appeared in the March/April 2006 issue of *I.D.* "汉字 Welcome" appeared as "Suspicious Characters" in the June 2008 *I.D.* "Left Wanting" appeared in the January/February 2007 *I.D.* as well as the anthology *Designing Magazines,* published by Allworth Press in 2007. Some of the Live Well Now! materials first appeared in the spring 2007 issue of *Opium Magazine.* "The Names in the Case," first published in the summer 2006 issue of *Hobart,* was named a notable essay in *Best American Essays 2007.*

TYPE CREDITS

The book text was set in Filosofia by Emigre. Emigre's Vendetta was used for the marginalia, headers, and footers. Fonts used in the second section include **Gloucester Extra Condensed** and **Twentieth Century**. The Chinese character set was SimSun. For "The Business of Design," the section titles were Americana, and the text was Goudy Old Style. Police reports used Letter Gothic, **Helvetica**, and Courier New.

IMAGE CREDITS

Most credits accompany the images. I took the photo of F. Clark Howell on page 30, the photos of the snakes on page 42, the photo of the alligator on page 64, and the photos of the book spreads on pages 56, 70, and 124. The rooster doodle on page 91 is mine. Mark Weiss provided permission to reprint his photo of liberal magazines on page 111 (www.markweissphotography.com). I scanned the business cards on pages 147, 149, 151, and 153. On page 170, the portraits of the characters Buck Masters and Tabitha Ert are sketches of criminals from the 1800s, reproduced in Stephen Jay Gould's 1981 *The Mismeasure of Man*. This book also provided two sketches for page 160: the brain sketch by E.A. Spitzka (1903) and the ape sketch reproduced from *Types of Mankind* (1854). On page 161, the character engraving comes from Shakespeare's *King Henry the Fourth, Part II* (1884). I took the photo for the hand puppet, page 164. On page 165, the star is a 1509 engraving of a dodecahedron designed by Leonardo da Vinci. The vector illustrations on pages 165 and 168 are mine. On page 169, bottom, the illustration of the mechanical chess player is from David Brewster's *Letters on Natural Magic* (1834). A patent illustration for magnetic-resonance imaging (1974) appears on page 165; for the personal stereo (1977), on page 168. On page 171, the lithograph of the calf with cyclopia is from the folio *Plates Demonstrating Normal and Abnormal Development in Man and Mammals* (1844–1849) by Willem Vrolik. On page 172, the illustration of the Monster of Ravenna (1512) is from Ulisse Aldrovandi's *Monstrorum Historia* (1642). On page 172, the figure on fire is a detail from Sandro Botticelli's illustration (1490s) of Dante Alighieri's *Inferno* (Dante wrote the *Divine Comedy* between 1308 and his death in 1321). On page 173, the portrait of Philip IV of Spain dates from the 1600s. The two surveillance photos on the next page were taken by my mother, Corinne Barringer.

STRATFORD POLICE DEPARTMENT
100 WILLIAM ROAD, STRATFORD, GD DS209-1C

SUSPECT
PROFILE

SUSPECT STATS

Be as specific and detailed as possible.

SUSPECT INFORMATION

NAME (LAST, FIRST, MI)
BARRINGER, DAVID

dlbarringer@gmail.com

TOWN/CITY   STATE   www.davidbarringer.com
Davidson, NC

DATE OF BIRTH 99069
CITY OF BIRTH   Chicago, IL
SPD FILE # 00-069-DB
STATUS: investigation authorized

☒ INDIVIDUAL   ☐ FINANCIAL ☐ BUSINESS
☐ GOVERNMENT ☐ AUTOMOTIVE ☐ COMMITTEE ☐ UNION
☐ NON-PROFIT   ☐ OTHER ORGANIZATION

ACTIVITIES: ☒ BOOKS   ☒ MAGAZINES   ☒ STORIES
            ☒ NOVELS   ☒ ESSAYS   ☒ BOOKLETS
            ☐ LAW   ☐ POETRY   ☒ SPECIAL PROJECTS
            ☒ MAKES & SELLS STUFF   ☒ PRINT COLLATERAL
            ☒ OTHER yes

EMPLOYMENT

CURRENT CLASSIFICATION
          DESIGNER/WRITER/PHOTOGRAPHER

ADDITIONAL CLASSIFICATIONS
writes/designs books, magazines, etc.

INDUSTRIES SERVED: ☒ AUTO ☒ UNION ☒ LEGAL ☒ SPEECH
☒ LITERARY ☒ MAGAZINES ☒ PUBLISHING ☒ GOVT ☒ CIVIC
GROUP ☒ NONPROFIT ☒ NEWSPAPER   ☒ OTHER_____

SUMMARY OF ACTIVITIES

A graduate of the University of Michigan and the University of Michigan Law School, Barringer was a freelance journalist in his twenties (writing for *The ABA Journal, The American Prospect, Details, Mademoiselle, Men's Journal, Men's Fitness, Playboy,* and others) until he was hired by [CONTD ON PAGE 2>]

PROFILE PHOTOS

Place two (2) or more images in spaces below

SPD-5 rev. 08/2008

STRATFORD POLICE DEPARTMENT
100 WILLIAM ROAD, STRATFORD, GD DS209-1C

SUSPECT
PROFILE

PAGE TWO (2) OF SUSPECT PROFILE:
BARRINGER, DAVID

a creative design and print company in Detroit. Barringer has written
two novels: **American Home Life** (2007) and **Johnny Red** (2005). His long
essay on graphic design **American Mutt Barks in the Yard** was published
in February 2005 as issue 68 of the graphic design journal *Emigre*.

Barringer has written for *I.D.*, AIGA's *Voice, Eye, The New York Times*,
and others. He was the recipient of the 2008 Winterhouse Award for
Design Writing and Criticism. He created the **Dead Bug Funeral Kit**.
He designs and is senior editor of *Opium* magazine. He is now based in
the Charlotte area of North Carolina but continues to work for seedy
characters in Detroit, New York, Portland, San Francisco, etc.

>>CONSIDERED DANGEROUS when not having a good work day. Recovered
emails expressing love to family, mother, brothers Dan & Mike--thanks
for all past and continuing conspiracies to John and Pat Rubadeau,
David Keeps, Roger Robinson, Lawrence Garcia, Rudy VanderLans, Steven
Heller, Julie Lasky, Todd Zuniga, Elizabeth Koch, Todd Neff, Jackie
Corley--and to readers Ghazaleh, Cathy, Kristin, Allison, Faruk, Felix,
Nick, Reeves, and so many others, as well as to members of The Davidson
Dog Park Club.

>>POTENTIAL TO CAUSE FUTURE HARM TO SELF AND/OR OTHERS is high, by
means of forthcoming novel about magazine designer, the monograph of
Nardo Gray, and who knows what else.

SIGNATURE OF OFFICER:

DATE: april 1, 2008

SPD-5 rev. 08/2008